DIXIE DAYS

DIXIE DAYS
Reminiscences Of A Southern Boyhood

Garry Bowers

A collection of amusing, witty and most often hilarious tales about fishin', huntin', campin' and growin' up in the 50's and 60's.

Shotwell Publishing

Columbia, So. Carolina

Dixie Days: Reminiscences Of A Southern Boyhood

©Copyright 2018, 2020 by Garry Bowers

The reproduction of this manuscript or any part thereof is denied without the express written consent of the author, who may be contacted via the U.S. Postal Service at 19 Lilac Lane, Montgomery, Al 36109

Produced in the Republic of South Carolina by

SHOTWELL PUBLISHING LLC
Post Office Box 2592
Columbia, So. Carolina 29202

www.ShotwellPublishing.com

ISBN: 978-1-947660-40-3

10 9 8 7 6 5 4 3 2

CONTENTS

INTRODUCTION vii

BOWHUNTING 101 1

THE DARK SIDE 5

THE SINGLE SEAT TWO WHEEL DRIVE
NON MOTORIZED ALL TERRAIN VEHICLE 7

THE BEST LAID PLANS 13

RX 17

MAC AND THE GREAT TREE 19

FOXES AND HOUNDS 25

THE WABASH EXPRESS 29

PITFALLS 33

CAMPING 101 37

HOW TO ROPE A BULLY 45

LESSONS LEARNED AT THE STATE FAIR 49

SNOW DAYS 53

THE DAM RIVER RATS 57

THE DANG BB BANGERS 61

BIKER BOYS	65
PHOBIA	71
GUNS 'N RODS 'N ROSES	75
PALE FACES	79
RED FACES	81
HISSSS	83
WHATEVER HAPPENED TO RANDOLF SCOTT?	85
ABOUT THE AUTHOR	89

INTRODUCTION

It was a whole different world when I was a kid. If you are a millennial, go play with your laptop because you are neither going to believe, understand nor appreciate this. There were no computers or cell phones. There were only two channels on your black and white TV. Your rotary phone had a party line, so you might have to listen to Maude from up the street explain to Lucille from down the street how to properly go about canning figs before you got to use it.

There were no plastic water bottles. If you were outside, you drank from the nearest garden hose. Nobody locked their doors. Ever. Most everyone went to church. Doctors made house calls. In Jr. High, our most forbidden and clandestine deed was smoking rabbit tobacco. If you were lucky enough to have a vehicle to drive to high school, you had a shotgun or deer rifle in it.

There were no school shootings or seat belts or R-rated movies. Very few folks had air conditioners. Everybody had a fireplace and the amount of wood stacked on the side of your house was an indicator of how good a provider the man of the house was. Political correctness did not exist. And we had not set foot on the moon. But we had Roy Rogers.

When I was a kid, except for school, you spent most of your waking hours outside. Mostly in pursuit of fishing, hunting, camping, exploring, etc. We played on the school football team until we figured out how to catch bass in cold weather. Many of our adventures were borne of sheer gumption and gross naiveté. Somehow and somewhat surprisingly, we lived. Despite the fact we had polio epidemics, starched jeans and Black Draught Cough Syrup. And we learned. Like I said, it was a whole different world back then. And in many ways, a much better one.

Garry

Chapter One

BOWHUNTING 101

I have recently experienced a curious phenomenon. Since I have retired, my wife is getting more and more supportive of my outdoor activities. With each passing week, she encourages me to go fishing, hunting, camping, etc. at every opportunity. I thought maybe it was my imagination, so just testing, I said one day, "I've been thinking about going bear hunting with a pocket knife this weekend". She asked how long I would be gone. "Really? That's what you want to know?" (I said to myself).

Ducky Jones, my lifelong friend with whom I grew up, was over the other day and as we sat in the den talking, he suggested I take up bow hunting. My wife, listening from the kitchen, gasped in delight. He told me it would significantly increase the number of deer hunting days and it was much more challenging than gun hunting. The whole time we were talking, my wife was yelling, "That sounds like fun, honey!" "What a wonderful idea!" "That sounds so exciting, it almost makes me want to go!" I was cringing. "I'll tell you where you can go." (I said to myself).

Anyway, Ducky began to list the equipment I would need. Compound bow, bladed arrows, practice target, target arrows, tree climber, stand, range finder, bow hunting techniques CD etc etc. I was doing some calculations in my head and quickly determined that venison taken by bow and arrow would cost approximately $32 a pound.

When I told him that sounded a little too expensive for my blood, my wife burst into tears, ran into the den and sobbed, "We can take out a second mortgage!" I ignored her. As she sniffled back to the bedroom to plan how not to speak to me for the next three days, Ducky asked, "Do you remember when we used to go bow hunting?" Even though we were born shortly after the dinosaurs became extinct, I remembered our preteen excursions all too well. We sat by the fire and reminisced.

Once a bunch of 10 or so year olds, went to the Canyon on a grand hunting expedition. The Canyon was actually a gravel excavation pit that juxtaposed the plateau upon which our little community sat and beyond it, the land dropped off rapidly to the northern part of the main town. You could see forever up there. It had the grandeur required of young explorers and frontiersmen and it was a perfect place for our hunting strategy that day.

Our quarry that autumn afternoon was the tens of thousands of migrating blackbirds that fly in massive flocks that time of year. Our weapons were bows and arrows. We weren't old enough for real guns and air rifles weren't powerful enough, but archery was good enough for the Indians, so it was good enough for us. The bows were a motley lot. Some were store bought plastics which you could pick up for the price of a few well mown lawns. Some were made by older brothers in shop class. One, as I recall, was a real adult hunting weapon which Ronnie had "borrowed" from his father. It was taller than he was and must have had an 80 pound pull, for he could only move the string about 2 inches. But it was impressive, and when you're 10 years old, impressive is what you go for.

There 7 or 8 of us and we lined up on the uppermost bluff of the gravel…I mean Canyon, and waited as the huge flocks of raucous birds neared the edge where we stood. Someone would count to three and we would fire in unison at about a 45 degree angle. To our great surprise, the stupid birds simply moved apart as our arrows reached their level and passed harmlessly through the resulting hole in the black cloud.

Since most of us had only one or two functioning arrows anyway, we had to climb down the nearly vertical 40 foot Canyon wall, go to the middle of the pit…I mean Canyon floor and pick up our projectiles. Then we had to climb all the way back to the rim in order to maintain the height advantage. After a half dozen times, it slowly dawned on us that the birds were going to split up every time we fired at them.

As we sat on the edge of the cliff, nearing arrow retrieval exhaustion, some genius said, "If we shoot straight up…(pant)… before the birds get here…(wheeze)…by the time they pass over us… (gasp)…the arrows will be coming down on them…(puff)…and they won't see them…" each little preadolescent mind absorbed this idea through a haze of oxygen deprivation and unanimously determined it to be a brilliant concept.

As the next wave of blackbirds approached, we drew taut our bowstrings (except Ronnie, who was barely able to move his), aimed straight up and calculated an algebraic equation involving the speed, altitude and distance of the flock and the trajectory and velocity of the target arrows so as to fire at precisely the correct moment. (Actually, someone just yelled "Now!") We released our arrows more or less at the same time. Miraculously the arrows slowed, reached their pinnacle, turned and began to fall back earthward precisely as the great mass of birds flew underneath them.

We had failed to factor into our theorem that if blackbirds could see 'down', they could see 'up'. The inevitable holes in the flock opened and again, the arrows went harmlessly through. Our disappointment was short lived though as it began to occur to us that we now had 7 or so very sharp, accelerating feathered missiles raining straight down upon us. Inside each little head, what passed for a brain strained mightily to connect synapses and form a complete thought. None came.

Being of single mind, we gave up trying to comprehend our predicament and turned ourselves over to primal instinct. Years later, my Grandmother would succinctly lace that feeling into poetic form: "When in danger, fear of doubt, run in circles, scream and shout." It was as if some great comedic deity had kicked over an ant bed. There was lots of scurrying around, but no one actually went anywhere.

That is, except Leonard, the more intelligent of our group, who chose to run in a straight line. Unfortunately, it was over the cliff. For me, the space-time continuum slowed to a crawl, as it has often done in my life in times of crises, so I can distinctly remember with vivid clarity portions of that disturbing scene. I know I probably watched too many cartoons as a kid, but I swear he actually hovered in mid-air for a moment, legs churning, before he plummeted out of sight.

And I saw Ronnie run directly into a rather large oak tree. I never understood that. It was as if he had no inkling that it was there. Or he had gone suddenly blind. Ricky's knees gave way and he just sat down in place, quivering. Then he did something strange. He covered his ears. I never understood that either. Granted, the air was rent with screeches and shrieks, most calling on Mama or God. But even covered ears could discern the "thunk" of descending arrows burying themselves in the ground all around us. Seconds apart. It seemed like hours.

Afterwards, Leonard, proudly displaying bloody contusions, ascended the cliff. Ronnie slowly regained groggy consciousness. Ricky babbled unintelligibly for a while, until his eyes became unglazed and he became coherent. We all just sat there, looking in amazement at the proximity of the arrows, as straight as little tombstones. Then someone said, "Hey, let's do that again!" And we all knew we would.

After Ducky's visit, I decided to give my wife a break from my presence, and went to the sporting goods store, just to price some bows and arrows. She mouthed a silent "thank you" as I went out the door. After confirming my suspicions about the price of the stuff, I ended up with a spool of monofilament. While standing in the checkout line, I overheard a young married couple in front of me talking about their kids. They were half-bemoaning, half-laughing about the dumb, dangerous antics of their children. They wondered aloud how those youngsters would survive to adulthood, given their recklessness and seeming lack of intelligence.

After listening for a while, I was appalled at the examples they gave of their offspring's idiocy. I finally said, "Guys, guys, guys. That stuff isn't stupid and your kids aren't ignorant. As a matter of fact, they're downright gifted!"

Chapter Two

THE DARK SIDE

I have never hunted at night. As far as I know, the only game that can be legally pursued in the darkness is the coon. And I am not going coon hunting. The adherents of that particular sport suffer from severe mental illness. The words "gun" and "flashlight" should never appear in the same sentence.

Someone invited me to go coon hunting once. When I declined, he said, and I quote, "You don't know whut yore missin'. Them blue ticks shore do bark purty." I started to ask him if his parents had the same last name before they got married, but I doubt he would have understood the question.

If I go into a swampy, snake infested, mosquito ridden, tick farm at night, it will be on the direct orders of the Lord Almighty. And even then, I would howl. I once walked in on my mother-in-law as she was getting out of the shower. (I didn't go blind, but I had to wear glasses for a while.) I would rather repeat that scenario than go coon hunting.

When I was a kid, though, nighttime and hunting did coincide. It had nothing to do with actually hunting at night, but the incident caused me to experience PTSD for several years, so it is worth mentioning. As was our annual habit, a bunch of us preadolescent Cub Scouts went on a charity drive in the neighborhood to collect canned goods for the local food bank. Parenthetically, we proved that coincidences are nothing more than grand cosmic jokes.

Not two minutes before we went up to the Johnson's house and climbed the steps up onto their large porch, Mr. Johnson, returning from a day of deer hunting, had pulled into the driveway and parked on the side of the house. It was almost dark. Had he been 60 seconds earlier or 60 seconds later, he would have not been following directly behind us, completely without our knowledge, as we rang the doorbell. He was still wearing his gillie suit.

When Mrs. Johnson came walking to the door, her kind smile quickly turned to a frown and she fairly yelled, over our heads, "You're late!" nine little Cub Scout caps turned in unison to see who she was talking to. A couple of the kids later confided they thought it was Bigfoot. A few were positive it was the Swamp Thing. I was personally convinced it was a disheveled grizzly bear, possibly rabid.

Kids left that porch in varying degrees of proficiency. Some jumped off, some stumbled and rolled off and some simply fell off. Ronnie clawed through the screen door with his bare hands and ran past a somewhat startled Mrs. Johnson. I temporarily stood frozen in nauseous horror. I know I didn't scream because I couldn't breathe.

When my legs spontaneously started working again, I ran the length of the porch and did a beautiful header off of the end. As I sprinted down the driveway, I noticed Fred engaged in valiant combat with a rose bush which had grabbed him as he ran by. I yelled words of encouragement as I passed him. When you're a kid, many things surpass loyalty. Overwhelming dread is one of them.

We gradually regrouped under the only streetlight on the block a few doors down from the Johnson's. When Fred walked up, scratched and bleeding, someone asked him where Ronnie was. Fred said, "I think it ate him". Little Jimmy made a whimpering sound and the front of his uniform pants turned a darker blue than they were supposed to be.

Fred was wrong because Ronnie showed up at school the next day. We asked him what had happened in the house, but he had lost all of his vocal abilities. As a matter of fact, he didn't speak a word for a week. My Mom said it was called "Hysterical paralysis". She might as well have said "Pissterical hilarious". I was in the 5th grade, for God's sake. Anyway, Ronnie was the only kid in school with snow white hair. To this day, when I see a gillie suit, I shudder.

Chapter Three

THE SINGLE SEAT TWO WHEEL DRIVE NON MOTORIZED ALL TERRAIN VEHICLE

No matter what you use these days to get to your hunting or fishing destinations, be it a 4 wheeler or a 4x4 or an SUV or a Hummer or (like me) a 40 year old army surplus jeep, your first sporting vehicle and instrument of freedom was probably a bicycle. Of course, we're not talking about the kinds of bikes they have today with all kinds of accessories, including speed switches, multi-diameter sprockets, speedometers, calorie counters, water bottles, lights, repair kits, safety stirrups, decorator logos, etc. etc. And, for heaven's sake, helmets! The only time a self-respecting kid in my neighborhood wore a helmet was on a football field. And they were made of compressed cardboard. I suppose that is a commentary on the sissyfication of America.

Anyway, most of the bikes today cost more than my jeep. Of course, groceries sometimes cost more than my jeep. Granted I was born shortly after the mastodons became extinct, but our SS 2WD NM ATV's were just bikes. Period. They were all red (sometimes, red orange, also called rust), with a frame, two wheels, a sprocket, a chain, a set of handlebars, pedals and sometimes, fenders. Usually, there was a seat also, but that was only on the newer models for kids normally got only one bike in their lifetime and for some reason, the seat went into complete degeneration about the third year, so those with older bikes had to stand and pedal. You only forgot not to sit down once.

Except for flat surfaces, all of our bikes were two speeds. Very slow uphill and very fast downhill. Uphill was the most painful speed. After the seat the next thing to wear out were the pedals. You would be gleefully riding along one day and the rubber part of the pedals would simply deteriorate and vanish, leaving you to brace on the little round, rolling bar for locomotion. And since there was some kind of law in those days (I believe it was called "parental") that forbade you to ride your bike in either your Sunday shoes or your school shoes, you rode barefooted because there was also a law against owning more than two pair of shoes. That really didn't matter, because after riding barefoot for a while, all the skin was gone off your toes and you couldn't wear shoes anyway.

Resting your entire body weight onto approximately one square inch of revolving metal on the second most sensitive part of your body (the bottoms of your bare feet) was not pleasant. However, on an older bike, you couldn't sit down to take the pressure off of your feet or the first most sensitive part of your body became involved.

The second speed (downhill) was not painful at all because the third thing that went out on your once-in-a-lifetime bike were the brakes. The idea that you were hurdling at breakneck speed and did not know how you were going to stop sort of desensitized your body. You no longer felt the excruciating pain in the bottom of your feet. Heck, if you were going really fast, you could even sit down.

There were only a few fishing spots within pedaling distance of our suburban neighborhood. The six or seven of us who hung out together would go to one of them every chance we got. We would tie our two piece spin casting rods and reels onto the handlebars, stuff a few plastic worms or live worms into our pockets and off we would go. We had the choice of a 5 acre pond in a strip mine pit, a year round branch with a few 3 foot deep holes in it and our favorite, some water hazards on a nearby golf course. Our favorite, that is, until one fateful autumn afternoon.

Of course, the country club/golf course was private property reserved for the rich and famous and the preteen scallions from the less economically fortunate surrounding neighborhood were not welcomed there. No problem. We just rode our bikes through the woods bordering the back nine, dismounted, and scurried down to the tiny ponds on or by the fairways. If it were the weekend, we would make a few desperate casts until someone spotted golfers coming toward us and then we would scramble back to the woods and wait for them to pass. The club was closed on Tuesdays, so we pretty much had free rein after school on that day, were it not for our nemesis, Willie the groundskeeper.

Willie was a large grizzled old man with long white hair and beard and he was always scowling and scanning the horizon. We had several close calls with him, but he had never gotten even nearly within grabbing range of us. We had always spotted him in time and made it back to the safety of the woods and the bikes. But one very windy Tuesday, we hadn't heard his tractor until he was almost upon us. We didn't have time to run our usual escape route, so instead chose to crawl up under a huge clump of pampas grass between the pond and the fairway. And that is precisely where Willie stopped. His assistant was standing on the trailer hitch and Willie half-turned to him and said in what I now know was a purposefully loud and staged statement, "I hope those kids aren't back down here fishing. I don't want to kill any more of them, but rules is rules". With that, he pulled out a pump shotgun with which he was famous for shooting gophers, and racked one into the chamber. The simple word "terror" does not begin to describe what seized us. There were only six of us but we broke and ran in nine different direction.

I don't think most people know this, but a panic stricken 10 year old can run approximately as fast as a cheetah, as I proved by crossing two fairways in about 6 seconds. I had reached a residential street off of club property, where I collapsed on my hands and knees, gasping for air. I listened for the sound of gunfire and screaming, wounded children, but heard nothing. All was deathly quiet except for some strange, muted distant laughter.

Happily, I walked home. It was good to be alive. We all went back the following day and retrieved our ATV's. Except for Fred.

The incident had shaken him so badly that he didn't go back for several days. When we started calling him "Fred, Fred, the scaredy head", he relented. Kids often respond positively to verbal abuse from their peers.

Needless to say, after our near-death experience, we didn't go back fishing at the golf course for a while. A couple of weeks later, we decided to visit the creek and armed ourselves with 3-piece fly rods and some popping bugs. It turned out to be another fateful day as our route took us down Dead Man's Hill. Now I know every neighborhood had one of these, but I defy anyone to show me one more foreboding than ours. It was a full two blocks long and far exceeded the limits of any road construction codes then in existence. The engineers had to have been drunk when they designed and built this monstrosity. The decline was about 60 degrees and the resulting bike speeds were close to the first quarter mile of a NASCAR race.

Anyway, me and Ducky Jones and a half-dozen other kids strapped our fishing gear onto our ATV's and headed out for a wonderful afternoon of creek fishing. About a block away from the Hill, some genius said, "I'll race ya'll!" When it comes to competition, one does not have to double-dog dare a ten-year-old. Those who were not already standing because they had no seat stood up and bore down on the pedals to get up a good head of steam.

We were almost even on Dead Man's Hill that day. At some point a little ways down that paved mountainside, I saw out of the corner of my eye (You didn't actually look away from the asphalt for fear of hitting a pebble and becoming airborne), that Ducky's front wheel was beginning to wobble. Like all good downhill racers, he was still pedaling furiously. Then a curious thing happened.

Ducky's SS 2WD NM ATV, apparently in a fit of depression over having no handlebar grips, seat, rubber pedals, or brakes, committed suicide. I heard the spokes begin to twang in rapid succession and in my peripheral vision saw the handle bars sag despondently. We were going so fast, the rust actually began to peel from the front fender. The chain jumped the speeding sprocket and the bike simply disintegrated.

Ducky let out the patented screech/squawk for which he was nicknamed and cars for several blocks around pulled over to wait for an emergency vehicle to pass. There was a loud thump and then, breaking several laws of physics, Ducky rolled past me in a little whirling ball from which occasional bits of checkered shirt, shards of metal, pieces of rubber and splinters of fiberglass fly rod flew. He arrived at the bottom of the Hill well before the rest of us, hampered as we were by the friction of tires on pavement.

He was just sitting there, almost naked, with huge eyes staring about incredulously. It was as if he had seen the Beyond. He looked like a skinned squirrel. If there was a piece of intact hide left on him, I didn't see it. A couple of the guys actually gagged. Except for that, there was total silence. We all instinctively knew we had just witnessed an event that would be talked about for generations.

The passage of time would be measured by this incident. Many decades later perhaps, someone would ask, "Do you remember that time the Baptist Church youth football team beat the Methodist team?" "Why yes. That was three weeks after Ducky Jones rolled down the Hill." Or, "When did you and your wife meet?" "It was exactly 7 years and 6 months after Ducky Jones' wreck."

As Ducky sat there, he said something amazing. "Is my bike alright?" A glance up the Hill pretty much answered that question. It looked as if someone had strewn the contents of a mechanic shop's garbage can onto the road. Some future EMT in our group, wanting to check his mental faculties, asked, "Who is the Vice President of the United States?" Ducky answered, "Millard Fillmore?" Since none of us knew anyway, we assumed he was correct and breathed a sigh of relief.

Someone had found a discarded cardboard appliance box on the side of the road and we slid it under him. No one actually wanted to touch him. We drug him home, placed him at the bottom of the steps, rang the doorbell and ran. Kids don't like to explain things to adults. I do remember that the healing process took the better part of the school year and his nickname was changed to "Scabby" for a while. And he wasn't allowed to be around kindergartners or small animals.

Despite our minor setbacks, our SS 2WD NM ATV days were true freedom. When you got home and Mom said, "Young man, where have you been?", you simply said "Fishin'!" No one could argue with "Fishin'". I don't think I've ever been as free since.

Chapter Four

THE BEST LAID PLANS . . .

Everyone who knows the outdoors understands that a successful fishing, hunting or camping trip is dependent upon preparation, organization and development. Even the short, simple excursions, which were the hallmark of our little gang of elementary school enthusiasts, were dependent upon planning.

Both the fifth and sixth graders had lunch at the same time, so that incorporated our whole group and we could sit at the same table and for the only time during the school day, could talk out loud without getting our knuckles or heads rapped with a yardstick.

We planned our excursions down to the most minute detail. Who, what, where, when and how. It could have been an after school bicycle ride to the creek to gig frogs or it could have been a march to the Canyon to camp all night. Regardless, there was as much planning as WWII battle plan. And therein lay the problem. Lunchrooms back in those days were not the carefree, joyful and raucous lunchrooms of today.

There was a sort of pall that hung over those cafeterias. In our short meetings, we had to surreptitiously dispose of our food while watching out for ever vigilant teachers and lunchroom personnel and simultaneously avoid the sights and sounds of nauseous and retching children so as not to become one and at the same time evolve effective scenarios that would make our trips successful. It was difficult to work under those circumstances.

Let me explain.

I just don't understand how kids today can complain about school lunches. They have pizza and hot dogs and burgers and fries and all kinds of really good junk food. When I was a kid, immediately following the Pleistocene Age, there was none of that stuff. We had green beans, meat and warm milk. That was it. Every day.

Sometimes they would try to disguise it and put the beans in a blender or burn the meat into a smoldering black disc. Once a guy who had already eaten was passing by the serving line in which I stood and threw up right In front of me. You have to understand that lunchroom regurgitation was common in those days. The quality of the food was such that if did not give its digester any warning, such as nausea or queasiness. It was just in your stomach one second and on the floor the next.

The really troubling thing about this incident, though, was that the disgusting spectacle on the tile floor in front of me was identical to the meal on my tray. I don't mean similar. I mean identical. Back then, girls did not squeal and boys did not point and laugh, for merely looking could set off a chain reaction barf that once incapacitated half the fifth grade. We almost set a school record that day.

There were no protests. The parent's reaction to complaints consisted of "Children in Europe are starving". I once made the ill advised suggestion that I send them my lunches. Once. And kids dared not express discontent to the lunchroom personnel. Behind the counter were always two or three very stern women (well, female hominids).

One usually weighed slightly less than a sumo wrestler and could bore completely through a terrified elementary student with her glaring set of close knit pig eyes. Another was 6'2" and had a horse face whose central attraction was a mouth full of long, scraggly, discolored teeth. She was always armed with a three foot metal spoon. I think she ate some of the smaller children.

Occasionally, some doofus would inquire of those ladies, "What's this?" One would snarl, "Stuff. Move on." The kid idiotic enough to ask again usually carried a metal spoon welt somewhere on his upper torso for several days.

We never had choices of fruit drinks, juice or tea. We always got milk. Always. And it came from a cooler that had never worked, so in winter it was warm; in the fall and spring it was hot. Of course, that went real well with undercooked green beans and overcooked meat. Especially if the milk had been delivered on Friday for Monday's lunch. To this day, I eat breakfast cereal dry.

However, the milk cartons were vital. See, a teacher stood by the sink window to which everyone brought their trays when they were finished. I always secretly suspected that her presence was to prevent us from being snatched into the kitchen to God knows what grisly fate. The pretense, though, was to ensure that we had cleaned our plates. If they were not empty, you were declared sick and sent to the school nurse. The school nurse cured every ailment with a shot. She used an equine veterinarian's needle. Hence, it was of utmost importance that our trays be devoid of green beans and meat.

That's where the milk carton came in. Since the milk, regardless of the temperature, was the least difficult item to choke down, you drank it and stuffed the "food" (contents of the tray) into the carton, thereby giving the illusion that you had eaten everything. Those cartons, I am convinced, saved countless lives.

We never knew what the meat was. It had a strange texture, a stranger smell, and could vary in color from blood red to ebony black. There was a grandmotherly community volunteer at the end of the serving line taking up money. Someone just outright asked her one day what kind of meat it was. Two of the serving trolls looked askance at one another and burst into uncontrollable laughter, the fat one shaking droplets of sweat into the green beans. I think I saw a single tear in the cashier's eye.

The meat was malleable. There were only two Catholics in our whole school, but by government decree we were required to be served fish on Fridays. Those sadistic women may not have been

French chefs, but they were creative. They simply molded the meat into the shape of a bluegill.

Once in a while, we were treated to dessert. It was always the same unsweetened apple sauce. Surprisingly, we found its consumption to neutralize the effects of sour milk.

So you can see that the planning of a fishing or hunting trip was not a smooth and simple procedure, uninterrupted by outside concerns. But somehow we got the job done. And things did get better in Junior High. We were even given a choice for lunch: gruel or swill. But that's another story. I saw a sign the other day that said "You are what you eat". If that's true, I'm in trouble. I know exactly what that makes me.

Chapter Five

RX

When I was a kid, I was a student in my spare time. Most of my life was occupied as a fisherman, hunter, camper, explorer, frontiersman and part time Indian tracker. As such, I had more than my fair share of injuries, wounds, impairments and illnesses. Considering that fact, the medicines in my house were extremely sparse, consisting of five items, three of which were not even medicines. And, my mom and dad had polar methods and means for cures and treatments.

Mom's remedies consisted mostly of ice, chicken soup and Grandma's recipe for a mysterious poultice. Strains, sprains and bruises were treated with an application of ice in a wash cloth. Childhood diseases such as measles, mumps and chickenpox were treated with chicken soup. And she purposely exposed me to those diseases. The idea was the quicker you contracted it, the sooner it would be over.

"Mom, I'm goin to the woodlot out back this morning." "Not so fast, young man. Ducky's mother tells me he has broken out in spots. We'll be going to pay him a visit today." Seriously? Seriously? Sure enough, I would contract whatever disease it was from whichever friend it was, be confined to bed for three days and fed chicken soup.

For any contusions, abrasions, or cuts short of an amputation, mom mixed up grandma's poultice in the sink and applied it liberally. Out of fear and concern for my emotional health, I never asked what was in it. I was scared "eye of toad and tail of newt" would be in the description. And it smelled...well, it smelled...indescribable. Think of sitting on a cow carcass and eating a hot souse meat sandwich on a summer day at a rendering plant. On more than one occasion, when she slathered it on my wound, I would pass out. Not from the pain, but from the stench.

Dad's cures consisted of two things: tobacco products and castor oil. The tobacco was fine and worked surprisingly well. For an earache, he would blow cigar smoke into the ear canal and then stop it up with a cotton ball. For bee stings or insect bites, he would apply wet chewing tobacco to the site. But his chronic use of castor oil was, and I cannot stress this enough, bordering on child abuse.

Aside from the afflictions which called for the use of Red Man or Tampa Nugget, virtually every other ailment he would attempt to cure with castor oil. No matter the complaint, he would say, "Boy, what you need is a good dose of castor oil." Please note that the words "good" and "castor oil" should never appear in the same sentence. It was the most vile, disgusting concoction man ever invented. If you've never had the opportunity to partake of it, the best way to describe the taste is a mixture of distilled tar, kerosene and rotted fish.

I will say this. One tablespoon would cause explosive diarrhea. But that's ok. A second tablespoon would cause immediate projectile vomiting. Dad labored under the illusion that a clean digestive tract was the cure to all mankind's ailments and injuries.

I learned at a very young age to hide any maladies, physical or microbial from my parents. If I fell out of a tree and punctured a lung, I would tell mom it was just a scratch. "Nothing some chicken soup won't take care of." And I could have been drug down the street on the undercarriage of a Buick and dad would eye me suspiciously and ask, "You feeling alright, son?" "Yeah, dad. Never felt better!"

I am convinced that downplaying and even ignoring my injuries is the reason I am able to smell and taste anything today.

Chapter Six

MAC AND THE GREAT TREE

When you were a pre-teen, your choice of hunting weapons was severely limited. Except when you went out to the country with your dad and used the old .410 single shot under close supervision, you couldn't use a real gun. It was frustrating, because we neighborhood kids had bunches of undeveloped woodlands right next to our community just chock full of small game.

Our BB guns wouldn't bring down a squirrel. And after what was referred to by our parents as "the gravel pit incident", all our bows and arrows had been summarily confiscated. They spoke of that event in hushed tones as they did not want everyone to know how intellectually deprived their kids were. It was actually just a blackbird hunting experiment involving arrow trajectory, but in adult retrospect, I can see how it could have possibly maimed or killed several 10-12 year old kids. And we would have preferred they had called it "the canyon episode". That would have been much more western moviesque. And "gravel pit" sounded so, I don't know, unfronterisman-like.

Anyway, with no viable weapons, all that local hunting land was going to waste. Until one summer day, I was walking down the street minding my own mindless business, when I caught movement out of the corner of my eye and almost immediately felt an excruciating, burning pain in my left shoulder that brought me to my knees. I would have screamed like a girl, except the sudden anguish had rendered my vocal chords inoperable.

After my initial shock, my first thought was that my left arm would have to be amputated. If I survived the blood loss. But I looked between the clenched fingers of my right hand clutching the wound and nothing was spurting out. Then I looked up at the grinning Ducky Jones standing in his front yard, eyes wide with glee. He shouted, "I found a squirrel killer!"

"What the hell did you shoot me with?!?" Then, realizing I was in the middle of the street, and knowing any overheard obscenities would be immediately reported to my parents, I said more quietly, "what *was* that?" Ducky held up a slingshot in one hand and a shiny green chinaberry in the other.

If you've never been hit by a green chinaberry launched from a 10 pound pull slingshot, you have no appreciation of life. The resulting agony is horrendous. Much like major surgery without anesthetic. It didn't take long before every kid in the neighborhood had visited the five and dime store downtown and was the proud owner of a 50 cent metal Acme slingshot.

Now, Ducky had the biggest chinaberry tree this side of Asia in his backyard. I'm talking huge! And that's where the 7 or 8 of us preadolescents gathered to try out our new weapons. We had gotten a whole bunch of cardboard boxes from behind the grocery store and drew squirrels on them. Well, actually, one looked like a hippopotamus, a couple favored crippled raccoons, and I swear one was identical to an aardvark I had seen in National Geographic. But they served the purpose. We might not have been very good artists, but we became decent shots in no time.

We realized, after shooting at the boxes for a while, that chinaberries would not bring down a squirrel. Someone said his older brother had suggested we use ball bearings for ammo in a real hunting situation. The next day, we priced them at the local hardware store and found they were the approximate price of gold nuggets, so we would have to save up for a while. Meanwhile, we would keep practicing.

Left to their own devices, 5th and 6th graders are not very good at carrying out organized practice or competition. It usually devolves into anarchy. So it was, at one session, when someone, I'm not saying who, planted a chinaberry squarely into the back of Ducky's skull. In an attempt at retaliation, Ducky missed his intended target and nailed someone else. It went downhill from there. The only thing that saved us from self-annihilation was the appearance of a teenager named Mac.

When he strode into the backyard, our chaos ceased. Teenagers and kids did not even acknowledge each other's existence back then, much less mingle. I think there was a legal statute about it. Yet, one was there in our very midst. It may have been my imagination, but I recall there was some Clint Eastwood western music playing in the background. He said simply, "I hear you guys are pretty good slingshootists". Now, there was a cool word with which we all could identify. Slingshootist. Yeah. We simultaneously nodded in the affirmative.

Mac reached into his back pocket and pulled out a custom carved shellacked oak weapon with doubled industrial rubber bands and a real leather pouch. It was at least a foot long. The flutes and Spanish guitars got louder. He said ominously, "you guys wanna have a real battle?" I volunteered, "Yeah, Mac. I'm on your side!" He scoffed, "No, I mean me against all of you. I get the tree". The gauntlet had been thrown down. In the interest of fairness and gross stupidity, we all agreed.

Mac was the smartest guy I ever knew. Actually, his IQ probably rivaled that of a fence post, but in the land of the blind, the one-eyed man is king. Speaking of which, Mac wore this pair of huge, thick glasses. They made him look like an owl on No-Doz. But he was brilliant. He knew that his slingshot was twice as powerful as ours and he grasped the concept of the demoralizing component of true pain. Chinaberries have the approximate consistency of pure titanium. When they are traveling at roughly the muzzle velocity of a deer rifle, they can do devastating damage not only to the human body, but the human psyche.

And we didn't even catch on to the fact that Mac got to get into the tree and that one can see out through the leaves, but one cannot see in through those same leaves. Nor did we ascertain that he would have an endless supply of ammo at his fingertips, whereas after we had used what we had in our pockets, we would have to charge the tree, endure countless direct hits from above, grab a handful of chinaberries and beat a hasty retreat, being pelted all the way back to cover. Mac was a genius.

Further, the Great tree, as it was thereafter known, was in the middle of a huge yard and the only cover for us was the back corners of the house and a shed on the edge of the lot. So Mac not only held the high ground, but he had unobstructed vision onto an open battlefield where there was no protection at all. His sagacity did not stop there.

We had reported to war in shorts, barefooted and maybe a cotton t-shirt. Mac was in blue jeans, boots and a flannel shirt. We secretly laughed at him, not quite grasping the idea that when he was actually hit by a lucky shot, it wouldn't hurt nearly as bad.

In one particularly vicious part of the battle in which Mac was in wonderful form and scoring rapid hits on every piece of bare skin that showed itself during the charges to replenish ammunition, one brilliant strategist decided what we needed was mobile cover while on open ground. Ronnie grabbed a garbage can lid, covered his head and upper torso and ventured into no-man's land.

Mac patiently waited until Ronnie was half-way to the tree. Then he loosed a succession of volley's that got Ronnie in both legs. Thwack! Thwack! Ronnie lowered to lid to protect his legs. Thwack! Stomach. Thwack! Left shoulder. Thwack! Forehead. And so on until Ronnie was reduced to a little knot of quivering agony lying in a fetal position under the garbage can lid. Bong! Bong! Went the deadly missiles against the metal. Trapped!

"Help, help, pleeeeease help!" whimpered our comrade. When you're 12 years old and pain in involved, fidelity doesn't mean much. We did cover our ears of muffle his piteous cries. The wails became groans, the groans became snivels and finally all sound from beneath the lid ceased. We all assumed Ronnie was dead. In a fit of vengeance, Bobby yelled, "Cover me!" and sprinted for the shed in the back corner of the yard. We all fired blindly into the tree as fast as we could while Bobby made his daring run. He only got clipped a couple of times and once safely inside the structure, he gave us the high-sign.

Mac could not hit him, but he let Bobby know he was in range. Ping! Pong! Went the chinaberries off of the little tin shed. Bobby was trapped. Whatever his initial plan had been, if indeed there had been one, was useless. Further, in the mid-afternoon sun, the temperature in the shed was only slightly less than the surface of Mercury. I recall you could actually see Bobby begin to melt. It was reminiscent of the Wicked Witch in the Wizard of Oz.

In an act borne of sheer desperation, choosing death by chinaberry rather than heat stroke, Bobby snatched up a discarded window screen from the shed and made a run back to the corner of the house, using the screen as a shield. The only thing that hurts worse than a chinaberry traveling at the speed of a meteor is one that has been fragmented through a window screen. Think of twenty simultaneous bee stings.

Splat! Splat! Bobby went down, screen and all. "Oooooowwwwww! Dang!" went Bobby. Splat! Splat! Went the berries. Two of our soldiers were now lying of the field. There was only one thing to do. Before we abandoned our friends, we decided to all step from around the house corner at the same time and all fire one last shot. Then we would run away. Whatever grisly end awaited our two comrades would just have to be chalked up to fate.

On the count of three, the rest of us stepped out and sent four chinaberries toward our unseen foe. What happened next was impossible, even from a theological standpoint. There was a greater possibility of my making straight A's in the 6th grade than of actually hitting Mac, much less disabling him. From the tree came an unearthly scream, "Cease fire! I give up! Can't see! Can't see!" The leaves shook and Mac half-dropped, half-fell to the ground. Two of our last shots had spattered dead center on each of his coke bottle lenses.

Let it be said that all kids have a killer instinct. Bobby rose from his stupor underneath the screen. Ronnie actually rose from the dead. All of us immediately surrounded Mac, slingshots fully drawn. "Surrender!" we yelled in unison. Mac, sensing rather than actually seeing us, and realizing his execution was imminent, held up his hands.

Oh, how we rejoiced! Mac the teenager was defeated! There we danced underneath the Great Tree, our heads covered with knots and our little bodies with huge red welts. We were victorious! Mac chuckled and walked off, cleaning his glasses. As we left the yard that day, I noticed a squirrel sitting on a fencepost in the corner of the yard, eyeing us suspiciously. I supposed there was some irony in there somewhere, but I was not smart enough to figure it out. We never did save up enough money to buy any ball bearings.

But I learned a lot about life that day. #1. When someone is in trouble, thank the Good Lord it's not you. #2. Nothing hurts like pain. #3. Just because you won doesn't mean you didn't lose. #4. Eyeglasses aren't necessarily a bad thing. #5. (One I use in my deer hunting strategy to this day). Get in the tree. Always get in the tree.

Chapter Seven

FOXES AND HOUNDS

When I was 12 years old or so, my folks occasionally dropped me off at my uncle's farm/ranch up in the country a couple of hours away. I have long since forgotten the *excuse* for doing so, but the *reason* was that I was 12 years old. Sane parents get away from their 12 year old boys whenever they can if they want to remain sane.

That lesson was driven home once when I invited my friend Ducky Jones to go with me one weekend. His mom walked him to the car and exchanged pleasantries with my parents as he climbed into the back seat with me. I noticed that she was sniffing and dabbing her eyes with a hankie. I whispered to Ducky, "Man, your mom looks like she is really going to miss you". He didn't even look up and replied matter of factly, "Tears of joy".

Those were fun weekends. Once, Ducky and I decided to parachute off of my uncle's barn. We each got an old sheet from the house attic, somehow climbed onto the top of the barn from the hayloft, grabbed two corners of each piece of linen in each hand and Geronimo'd off. It should have worked. I still don't know how we miscalculated, but the sheets did not open. It may have had something to do with fundamental physics.

Ducky was, as usual, lucky and landed on a hay bale. I, on the other hand landed in the pig pen. Fortunately, a rather surprised 300 pound sow broke my fall. Otherwise, I might not have escaped with a simple concussion.

Consequently, I don't remember a great deal about the rest of that weekend. But I recall with vivid clarity one particularly exciting weekend right before Christmas that I went without Ducky. I participated in a style of hunting I had neither done before nor since. When we pulled up, Uncle was waiting on the porch, so my folks just let me out of the car and fled. Mom said in parting, "We'll pick you up Sunday night. Have fun and be careful". It was a rhetorical statement. She knew I would have fun because I was spending the weekend in the country. And she knew I would not be careful because I was, well, me.

I remember thinking to myself, "Well, which one do you want me to do? Have fun or be careful?" And then I thought quickly, "I hope I didn't say that out loud". See, in those days, that would have been designated as "sass" and a kid participating in "sass" would likely have been snatched up and beaten half to death. But she did not come flying out of the car window after me, so I assumed I had not actually verbalized those words.

Each night at supper, my uncle would regale me with tales from his childhood. And he had quite an imagination. I would sit in rapt attention, probably with my mouth half open and listen intently. He would ignore my aunt, who would roll her eyes and shake her head and occasionally say his first name as if she were scolding a child. On that one particular visit, I mentioned how cold it was and he scoffed at me. He said the weather was much, much colder when he was a kid and they had blizzards most every day during the school year.

He told me he had to walk to school each day through 4 feet of snow. Six miles. Uphill. And he had to walk back home each evening through 5 feet of snow. Seven miles. Uphill. The geographic impropriety of that situation never occurred to me at the time. Though my aunt didn't seem to enjoy his stories, I did. And he loved telling them.

After supper that night, we settled in front of the television. Even with the 60 foot antennae uncle had installed, we were so far from a broadcasting station, the little black and white set only picked up one channel. There was an old movie about the English aristocracy and it was soooo boring. Lots of adults with a funny accents talking about stuff I didn't understand. I think mostly politics and family disputes and (yuck) romance.

At one point, one of the characters told another that they had to "put petrol in the lorries". I asked what that meant. My uncle said "put gas in the trucks". I asked why didn't they just say that. He said, "It's a foreign film, son. They probably just don't speak English very well". "Oh", I said. My aunt got up and left the room.

But there was one respite. In the middle of the movie, was a real Royal British foxhunt, complete with galloping horses, a slew of running hounds and the blare of hunting horns. It made quite an impression on me. And there I was on a ranch with acres and acres of prime hunting land, horses and even a couple of old beagles.

I asked uncle if I could take one of the horses the next morning and hunt with his dogs. "Do you remember how to ride?" "Yes sir!" "Did you bring your gun?" "Yes sir!" It was a done deal. I could hardly wait. I didn't even dread sleeping in the attic that night. That was the location of the only extra bedroom in the rambling old farmhouse. It was unheated. In the winter, it was far, far beyond the simple word "cold". A polar bear would have been miserable up there.

When I crawled into the old iron bedstead that night, my aunt commenced covering me with about 80 pounds of quilts and blankets. I had to be in the position in which I wanted to sleep when she started because when she finished, I couldn't move. When I woke up the next morning, it took a good ten minutes to extricate myself from beneath the covers, but I was motivated, going on my first British foxhunt and all. I dressed and ran to the bathroom to check my nose for frostbite. Uncle met me in the barn after breakfast and saddled up a frisky 3 year old stallion for me. As creative as uncle was at spinning yarns, he had no such proclivity when it came to names. He called the horse "Fred" and both dogs were named "Dawg".

Anyway, I mounted up with my .410 single shot strapped to my back with a home-made sling. He called "Here Dawg. Here Dawg" and they both came running. Before I left, he warned, "Don't shoot from the saddle. Fred isn't used to guns. Dismount, tie him up and then do your shooting". I assured him I would. He then left to do some errands and I was off on my first British hunting expedition.

I thought it would be appropriate to give my mount a good English name and said, "Come on Dunbarton. Let's go slay some fox!" We crossed the pasture, or as I called it, the King's Royal Grasslands and were almost to the Gamekeeper's Forest, when the hounds jumped a fox. Well, a rabbit.

It should be noted here that an adult's memory can be measured in weeks, months and even years, according to the circumstances. For a pre-teen, memory retention on any subject is approximately 90 seconds. (I believe that has been scientifically proven). My uncle's admonition about not shooting from the saddle had taken place a full five minutes before, well outside the 90 second time frame. So, I unslung my little gun and fired.

My trusty steed came unglued. He levitated a full 18 inches, turned around in midair and headed at full speed back to the barn. I lost my shotgun, my reins, my breath and all control of my bodily functions. I did manage to keep one foot in a stirrup and both hands on the saddle horn. A terrified, galloping horse is neither a reliable nor comfortable means of transportation. Cowboys make it look easy in the movies, but I spent as much time in the air as in the saddle, behind the saddle and in front of the saddle. To use the British expression, let's just say it was a smashing ride. I was lucky to ever have children.

And somewhere in the recesses of my tiny 12 year old brain, I knew that a horseback rider had to bend over to leave through that particular barn door. I had done that just a few minutes before. For the life of me, I don't know how I assumed I did not have to duck on the way back in. But the 90 second rule had kicked in again.

I woke up in a pile of barnyard manure (some of it may have been mine) with a busted forehead and Dunbarton nuzzling me, ostensibly to see if I were still alive. I swear he was grinning. I try to gather some wisdom with each misadventure I have encountered. On that day, I learned why the Brits wear that silly hunting attire. Red jackets don't show blood and the little black caps cover up the knots on their heads. I suppose they would say of me, "He was a bit bonkers as a wee lad". And they would be right. Tally Ho anyway.

Chapter Eight

THE WABASH EXPRESS

My lifelong friend, Ducky Jones, and I were lamenting the state of today's kids recently. On beautiful warm weekends, they are actually indoors, by choice, hunched over a computer screen, killing robots in some silly fantasy game. How sad. I asked Ducky if he remembered one particular time when we were kids and got involved in carpentry and construction. He said, "Indeed I do. We were 11 years old". I asked how he could possibly remember our exact age in an event that occurred over a half century ago. "Because", he replied, "I distinctly recall thinking that I would not live to be 12 years old. Besides," he sheepishly admitted, "I still have nightmares about it".

The community in which we grew up sat on a plateau overlooking the rest of the town. The edge of our neighbor hood and said town were about a half mile apart and the elevation dropped several hundred feet between the two, leaving hundreds of acres of undeveloped, very, very steep woodland in between. To us kids, it was Disneyland. When not in school, we spent most of our waking hours there.

Deep down in the woods where the land began to flatten out again and civilization reappeared meandered a little creek, full of tiny, tasty bream. We kept a stash of cane poles there hidden in a hollow tree and we dug worms from the bank of the stream for bait. The problem was, it was a long way off. One day, Ricky, who lived on the street right across from the edge of the precipice, found a pair of old water skis in his dad's garage. (You know what's coming, right?)

Five or six of us were at Ricky's house on Friday after school and he brought out his newly discovered treasure. Some Einstein in our gang came up with an idea of how to get to our fishing hole faster: build a sled. To correctly estimate the intellect of a bunch of 5th and 6th graders, you have to consider that not a single pea-brain among us ever pondered how we would get the contraption back up the hill. Turns out, we didn't have to. (Don't get ahead of me.)

With a few 2x4's, a saw, a couple of hammers, a bucket of old nails, some discarded furniture and a surprising amount of juvenile ingenuity, in a few short hours we cobbled together a sled, not too much unlike the ones used in the Iditarod today. It was six feet long, four feet wide, and had a single 2x4 wooden seat in the front, followed by two double seats made from ancient wicker lawn chairs and a single 2x4 stand in the rear. It was a thing of beauty.

Since all the makings belonged to Ricky, he got to name it and came up with "Wabash Express", after a popular country song of the day entitled "Wabash Cannonball". Someone painted the name on the side of our project, and I am fairly sure it was misspelled because it consisted of two words of more than one syllable each. Anyway, we were proud. We agreed to meet early the next morning and take the Wabash Express on its maiden run to the creek.

The anticipated morning dawned cloudy and wet; since it had rained all night and the leaves covering the forest floor fairly glistened with moisture. We had made all kinds of trails in those woods and we moved our contraption across the street and placed it carefully in front of one such path on the last piece of level ground for half a mile.

Ricky, again being the great provider of materials, chose to sit on the single board in front. Ducky and Ronnie and Bobby and Bubblehead occupied the two wicker seats and I, being the tallest (and most naïve) of our group stood on the back brace. The trail was wide enough for the Express, but it took a right turn about 100 yards away. With only a minimal understanding of arithmetic and absolutely no knowledge of basic physics, we decided, after much strategical discussion, that we could all lean in that direction at the appropriate time and the sled would follow our lead. We were not very bright.

Had the TV show "Star Trek" not been years into the future, an apt opening line for our adventure that day would have been "Warp speed, Mr. Sulu". But Ricky just yelled "Go!" and I pushed us off. As soon as my foot left the ground, I said to myself, "My God, what have we done?" My Grandfather had an expression that perfectly described the condition of the trail that day. He would have said it was "as slick as a goat's butt". Having never examined that particular animal closely, I wouldn't know. But I would take Grandpa's word for it.

The friction between waxed wood and wet leaves can best be described as "minimal". In actuality, it was closer to "non-existent". Our speed increased exponentially and doubled approximately every 10 feet. We reached the curve in the trail in about 3 seconds after liftoff, and that just happens to be the estimated time it takes a kid to form a complete thought, so there was no leaning. We just flew off through the woods at breakneck speed. Between the Wabash Express and 6 kids, we weighed well over 500 pounds and ran over seedlings and small saplings like we were in a Sherman tank. Nary a bump. Larger saplings resulted in a small jolt.

I was waiting to hit a hundred year old oak and remember thinking that little Ricky would be the first to die, but only milliseconds before the rest of us. No one screamed. The air was rushing by so fast it was impossible to breathe in enough oxygen to make a sound. In the tunnel vision created by unspeakable horror, I spotted a log lying directly in our path up ahead, and being the self-preservationist that I am, I bailed out, backward. I landed on my rear and continued to follow the sled, feet first, about ten feet behind.

It is difficult to describe what happened when the sled hit the half-buried log. The best I can come up with is, it exploded. The Wabash Express came to an abrupt halt and disintegrated, to some extent on a molecular level. It simply ceased to exist. And we proved Newton's Law of Motion to be empirically correct to a scientific certainty. The sled stopped, but the kids kept on going. Ricky, sitting in front, was spit out like a dart through a blow gun and went in a straight line several feet off the ground and at terrifying speed.

When I hit the log, feet first, my spine should have been driven through the top of my skull. But God looks after kids and fools, so I was double covered that day. All the impact did was rattle my teeth and bring me to a sitting position where I had an excellent vantage point to watch the other 4 kids flailing about wildly through the air, in several directions, arms and legs flapping with abandon. Somehow, no one hit anything hard and no one was killed instantly. I don't know why.

When we all recovered our senses, we limped and hobbled down the hill to look for Ricky. There his carcass lay in a tangle of rusty barb wire, with cuts, hematomas, bruises and various contusions. In his sincere surprise to be alive, he mumbled several times, "I'm alright. I'm alright". Ducky stood there staring down at him and said in a strange, deadpan tone, "No you're not".

After gingerly and queasily extracting Ricky, we all started our trek back up the hill. On the way, someone spotted a pair of pants on a tree limb about 10 feet off the ground and for the first time we noticed Bobby did not have any jeans on. We stared upwards in awe at them for a moment and then walked on. Nobody cared. Not even Bobby. When we got back to the landing, I noticed Ronnie had a small, crooked stick jammed under his scalp on the side of his head and there was a little trickle of blood running down beside his ear. He looked like he was trying to grow an antler. Everyone was too tired to mention it. He would find out later.

Ricky had to get a tetanus shot or two and walked around for a few days looking like he had fallen face first into a porcupine. Bobby got a whipping for coming home with no pants. But boy, did we have a tale to tell at school. Kids today just don't know how to have fun!

Chapter Nine

PITFALLS

An outdoorsman's life is full of pitfalls. Especially when you're young The other day my lifelong friend Ducky Jones and I were reminiscing about our early school days. Our teacher, Mrs. Frumpett, was a master at intercepting the notes that were furiously passed back and forth every afternoon right before school let out.

She could be writing on the chalkboard with her back to the class and spot a note speeding from hand to hand as if she had been looking right at it the whole time. It was spooky. I often suspicioned she was a space alien. One afternoon, I passed one to Ducky reminding him of our fly fishing trip immediately after school. Mrs. Frumpett pounced on it just like I had raised my hand and told her I was going to do it.

How embarrassing! She made a big deal out of opening it and lowering her glasses to the tip of her nose. I assumed she was going to read it aloud and make some snide comment to cause us to turn redder than we already were. Instead, she gasped, grabbed us both up by our respective shirt collars and literally drug us to the principal's office.

All the note said was, "Don't forget this afternoon. Bring a couple of yellow poppers". Mrs. Frumpett, equating "poppers" with that era's equivalent of bennies, uppers and goof balls, assumed she had just busted an elementary school drug ring. Ducky and I, of course, did not have a clue what was happening. But fortunately, Mr. Cicero, the principal, knew us well and understood completely.

He explained to Mrs. Frumpett not only what popping bugs were, but gave her their entire piscatorial history beginning in the 19th century. She was totally flustered. Ducky and I just hung our heads and grinned. Mr. Cicero sent her back to class and assured her he would explain the evils of note passing to us two miscreants.

As soon as she left, he asked, "Where are you boys going fishing?" We told him we were headed down to the old strip mine pond. He frowned and asked, "Aren't there some 'Keep Out' signs down there?" Ducky said he was pretty sure those were just suggestions. Besides, they were old and rusty. Mr. Cicero winked, said, "You boys be careful" and dismissed us. Mr. Cicero was so cool.

When you are 12 years old, your philosophy of life is simple. Parents were put on earth to keep you from having any fun, so it was your job to do everything they told you not to do. My mom had told me never, ever, ever go to the strip mine pond, so it was my duty to go every chance I got. To keep me away, she told me the pond had pockets of quicksand all around it. Of course, I knew better because of my previous forays there, but couldn't disagree without telling on myself.

And she insinuated, should I step in said quicksand, I would be instantly sucked down into the bowels of hell where the devil would lecture me for eternity about the consequences of disobeying parents. Now, I had many times experienced mom's whippings with a cherry tree switch, so the quicksand alternative didn't sound all that bad.

Cherry tree switches are especially heinous devices because, stripped of their leaves, they have these hard little nodules on them and are comparable to a medieval cat-o-nine-tails. And the worst part was, I had to go to the cherry tree in the back yard, pick the instrument of torture myself and deliver it to her. "Go get another one. This one's too thin." Or, "This one's too short". Or, "This one won't draw blood." Picky, picky, picky. The dreaded "choosing of the switch" ceremony was a lot worse than the actual whipping.

Anyway, Ducky and I bicycled to the pond that afternoon, dismounted and headed down the trail to the water. It had rained every day that week and the path had turned into a bog. There was no quicksand, but there was a lot of quick mud. Before we got half way to the pond, I went up to my knees, floundered around like I was trying to exit a clown car, got covered in muck and lost both my shoes. We gave up any idea of fishing and headed home.

On the ride back, I considered pulling a George Washington and cutting down the cherry tree to prevent the inevitable whipping. I could drag it to the wood lot next door. Unlike George, however, I would lie my butt off about it.

But when I pulled into the yard, Mom was already standing on the front porch, arms folded, tapping her foot. She said, "Well, I can see who's not getting any birthday cake tonight!" In what passed for a brain in my silly young head, I slowly processed that sentence and realized it was my birthday! And Mom wasn't going to whip me on my birthday!

An outdoorsman's life is full of pitfalls. Some of the time, we can walk around them. Sometimes we can jump over them. But occasionally, when we actually tumble into one, it's really not so bad. That was the best birthday cake I never got to taste.

Chapter Ten

CAMPING 101

Camping today is more popular than it has ever been, with millions of Americans participating annually. I love it and often combine the activity with hunting and fishing trips. However, considering my early experiences, it is a wonder that I have a predilection for it at all.

I was four years old before I realized my name wasn't Nogarry. That trend continued throughout my young life.

"Mom, can we use the extension ladder to build a tree house?"

"Nogarry, you'll break your neck."

"Dad, can we use the chainsaw to build a log cabin?"

"Nogarry, you'll cut your legs off."

"Dad, Ronnie's dad will let us use his blowtorch if…"

"Nogarry, you'll go blind." (That's not the last time I heard that.)

Then, when I was about 12, things inexplicably changed.

"Mom and Dad, me and Ducky and Ricky and Bobby and Charlie and Ronnie and Bubblehead want to know if it would be alright to…"

"Nogarry." "Nogarry."

"...go camping tonight?"

"Camping?" "Where?"

"Down in the Canyon."

"You man that gravel pit behind Skyline Drive?"

"Well...yes sir."

"All night long?"

"Well...yes ma'am."

"That'll be fine. What time are you leaving?"

"About five o'clock this afternoon."

"Make it three."

It seems I had hit upon a recreation they agreed to. Always. Amazingly, so did my friends' parents. My folks even adding that we might want to devote an entire weekend to the activity.

Preparations for camping trips sometimes lasted almost as long as the trip itself. Like our predecessor frontiersmen whom we tried to emulate we became more proficient as we became more experienced. For instance, the first time we ventured into the great wilderness known as The Canyon (That name was said quietly and with reverence) at night, flashlight was number nine on our list, way down from BB guns (the place abounded with wild game) and bows and arrows (in case we ran out of BB's) and Kool-Aid (everyone in our group had his favorite flavor permanently etched on his upper lip).

However, after the first trip, number one on the list was many, many flashlights and number two was lots and lots of flashlight batteries. We had quickly discovered the true meaning of "dark". We're talking pitch-black-can't-see-your-hand-in-front-of-your-face-not-a-street-light-in-sight-dark. We gained great respect for Daniel Boone, him having to lug so many EverReady products around with him and all.

Knives were always on the lists. We never used them but somehow they seemed indispensable for a camping trip. I mean, just think about going camping without a knife. We never did figure out a purpose for them, but we know ol' Dan'l carried one on his belt, probably right next to his flashlight. We did sharpen them a lot though, and after a couple of trips, number three on our list was a first aid kit.

In the early days, our tents were in the experimental stage and something to behold. Our most impressive shelter, we built in Ronnie's backyard. It was a bed sheet tied to four metal lawn chairs. But we ran into a problem when his parents refused to let us take the furniture to The Canyon. Hypocritical people, Ronnie's parents. Loved for us to go camping, but not with their stupid wrought iron stuff.

Then we came up with the idea of sticking a pitchfork and a posthole digger in the ground, tying a length of rope between the two and draping a bed sheet over the rope. Then we pulled it taut and anchored it to the ground with the largest nails we could find. It looked just like a U.S. Army pup tent except for the fact that is was white with a floral design on the edges. General Patton be darned. It was a thing of beauty and it would protect us from the elements. That is, we later discovered, unless it rained or unless the wind blew or unless it turned cold.

That was no problem. We simply timed our excursions to coincide with favorable weather. Sometimes, though, we would fail to take into account a heavy morning dew and were awakened in the wee hours with our structure collapsing on us. You haven't lived until you've been snatched from a fitful sleep at 5 a.m. pummeled by garden tools and enveloped in a wet sheet. But we chalked that off to the wilderness experience. We were sure that sort of thing never discouraged Mr. Boone. Heck, he might not have even had a sheet. (If he did, it probably didn't have flowers on it.) Occasionally though, things went terribly wrong.

One absolutely beautiful Autumn Saturday afternoon, we took off for The Canyon looking forward to a night of primeval adventure. The seven or eight of us trudged through the neighborhood, struggling under the weight of our gear and supplies. Some of it had come from the Army surplus store. A couple of the guys had been fortunate enough to procure a couple of well oversized WWII helmets, which they wore with pride. Most of us toted one of the necessary long-handled garden implements which were the backbone of our tents.

Our canteens full of Kool-Aid sloshed and our belted knives clanked as we made our way to the great outdoors.

Ol' Man Jenkins yelled from his front porch rocking chair, "You boys going to the Great Farmin' War?" (I hated Ol'Man Jenkins.)

"Naw, Mr. Jenkins", Ronnie hollered back, "We're just going camping down in the Canyon".

"Well, you boys be careful. Watch out for Old Leo."

Our march slowed considerably. "Who's Old Leo?" asked Ronnie.

"Why, that wildcat that lives down yonder", Mr. Jenkins replied flatly, as if everybody knew about it.

We stopped in the middle of the street. Ronnie was sort of the spokesman for our group when dealing with adults, because he had the habit of stuttering when he got excited. We had figured out, through that seventh sense that kids have, that if we got into real trouble, people usually felt sorry for Ronnie and we would get off scot free.

"Wi, wi...wild-wild cat?" Ronnie stammered. We had moved up to the edge of the porch.

Mr. Jenkins studied a moment and said, "Well, I wouldn't call him a wild-wild cat. Just your average wild cat. But he's a mean 'un."

"Me, me, me..." Ronnie tried.

I took over. "Mean?"

"Yeah", said Mr. Jenkins. "Terrible mean. Downright vicious."

"You ever seen him, Mr. Jenkins?" I queried.

"Nooooooo, son. Wildcats is nocturnal creatures."

"Noc, noc", said Ronnie.

"Who's there?" asked Bobby.

"Shut up, Bobby", I said frantically. "Mr. Jenkins, what does nocturnal mean?"

He replied, "Them is animals that only feed at night. And I ain't never been down there at night. As a matter of fact, you wouldn't catch me dead down there at night".

That information perceptibly slowed our march to the gravel..., I mean Canyon. Ronnie's cadence had deteriorated to "hut, hut... hut wu, wu, wun" so he sounded more like a nervous quarterback than a drill sergeant and we looked like we were skipping rather than marching.

We finally made it to the site, though with barely an hour of daylight left. Just enough time to bury the heads of various garden tools into the ground and erect our bed sheet tents. Collectively, we agreed that since it was already late, we would set up camp near the dirt road entrance rather than near the woods which surrounded the Canyon on three sides. It seemed like the logical thing to do.

Strangely, there were no volunteers to go collect firewood. Since this was the most manly of camp chores, we normally fought over the job. But for some reason, a sort of suspicious lethargy prevailed that night. Since Bubblehead had earlier admitted he had forgotten the B-rations (beans and weenies), he was summarily selected to gather firewood if he wanted anything to eat.

Despite his protestations that he was not hungry, he was finally triple-dog-dared and had no choice. It was just as well, for Bubblehead was useless in setting up camp. He had gotten his nickname because he was forever chewing Bazooka gum and blowing bubbles. He invariably ended up with with a sticky residue on everything from his hands to his eyebrows to his clavicle and he stuck to everything with which he came into contact. He was, however, the best left-fielder I ever saw. He never dropped a fly ball and once even caught one with his forehead.

We had barely got the tents erected when Bubblehead returned from his foray in record time. He came scurrying across the Canyon floor, looking for twigs, small limbs, branches, leaves, pine straw and mulch. He carried and had it all stuck to him, like a trash pile with legs. Such had been his haste that, when he got to us, a disoriented chipmunk jumped from the debris that was attached to him.

Bubblehead gasped, "I think...I heard...Old Leo!"

"There's no such thing!" screamed Charlie, in a volume and manner reminiscent of a firing squad victim.

"Ol' Man Jenkins was just trying to scare us!" blurted Ricky, in complete denial.

"There's no wildcat down there!" quacked Ducky. His statement sounded suspiciously like a question.

"Yeah!" added Bobby. Bobby wasn't very articulate.

An uneasiness fell about the camp. The sun set rapidly. After three boxes of matches and lots of cursing ("damn" and "hell" were about the only cuss words we knew and they had a limited combination, but we were creative), we had a roaring fire and the smell of burning S-rations (canned spaghetti) wafted about the night air.

We had never quite gotten the hang of cooking canned food. We did learn after our first outing that the cans had to be opened before they were placed on the fire. Heated, unopened cans are not as loud as fragmentation grenades, but the resulting explosion is nonetheless surprising. Imagine squatting close to a large campfire, staring hypnotically at the blaze, anticipating a warm, well-deserved meal one second and the next second you are partially deaf and covered with scalding beans. A lesson well learned.

Our experience had taught us to open the cans first, but there was still the debate over when the food was done. There was the "label-burned-off" method, the "can-turned-black" method, and the "forgot-the-long-handled-pliers" method. The latter usually resulted in an inedible supper.

This particular night, after we choked down the meal, in varying degrees of scorched, there wasn't the usual round of stories involving ghosts, murderous hermits or grizzly bears. And everyone was very careful not to mention Old Leo. Instead, we started talking about the stars (you could actually see them in those days) and reflecting on their wonder. We decided they were at least a hundred miles away. And we discussed various theories about why they fell from the sky.

Bobby admitted he knew nothing about the stars. With much scoffing and derision, we pointed out various constellations to

Bobby. Over and over. But he just couldn't see them. We left him to his bewilderment.

Ricky cut his finger while sharpening his knife. We went into emergency medical technician mode. We laid him down, gave him a big slug of Kool-Aid, and then four guys held him while another doused the wound liberally with iodine and covered it with a big wad of bandages. Then, an ember from the fire floated down and caught Charlie's hair on fire. We doused him with Kool-Aid and threw handfuls of dirt on him. In the flickering firelight, he looked amazingly like a deranged coal miner.

But generally, everything was quiet and there was no real excitement. We began drifting off to the tents for a night of peaceful slumber. All except Bobby. He sat by the dying fire determined to find and identify one of the constellations we had pointed out to him. After a couple of obligatory tent evacuations (Never sleep with anyone who has consumed a pound of burnt spaghetti), things began to settle down.

Just as I was in that twilight between reality and dream, Bobby identified a star group. Though he was alone outside, in his surprise and enthusiasm, he fairly shouted, "Oh! Leo!" Guess what that sounded like? The initial flurry of activity could only be described as abandoned chaos.

In the ensuing seconds after Bobby had uttered those two words. The tents were ripped to shreds as unfathomable panic set in. Most simply ran in the direction they happened to be facing at the moment. A garden rake flipped and the tines caught Ricky squarely in the shins. "He's got meeeeee!" We ran away from Ricky's piteous wail. I picked up a pair of pliers instead of my trusty flashlight, pointed them in Ricky's direction and tried in futility to turn them on. I don't think it was so much bravery as an uncontrollable urge to witness the bloody carnage.

In the dying firelight, Ronnie sat perfectly outlined under a collapsed bed sheet. I suppose his reasoning was that if he couldn't see anything, it must not be happening. He was softly muttering, "Le...Le...Le".

Ducky stood near the fire in a crouched, defensive posture, knife in hand, cutting blindly at the air. He had forgotten to remove the scabbard, so when Bubblehead ran squarely into him, he wasn't cut to ribbons. Ducky, of course, assumed a sticky cat had attacked him. The air was rent with screeches of doom and hopelessness.

Various objects were thrown in Ricky's direction in hopes that he might be saved. His screams were suddenly silenced when he was hit in the head with a pair of pliers and a four-battery flashlight. All sound abruptly ceased except for fading footsteps and the diminishing monotone of "Le…Le…Le". I was suddenly alone. Ricky was obviously dead, so there was nothing left for me to do there. I, too, was in my own bed at home in less than 10 minutes.

The neighborhood was somewhat in awe the next morning. People stood speechless in their yards, wondering how the streets, literally overnight, had become cluttered with tennis shoes, knives, canteens, helmets, pieces of bed sheet, flashlights and the occasional pair of soiled underwear.

Today, when I see kids in my neighborhood preparing for a camping trip, I tell them the story of our brave stand against a pack of mountain lions down in the Canyon. I encourage them to go camping. And I always mention that there are probably not even any wildcats around anymore. Except for Old Leo.

Chapter Eleven

HOW TO ROPE A BULLY

No, this has nothing to do with the rodeo. It has become wildly popular as of late to attack school bullying. They have taken out TV ads, flooded social media with dire warnings and even held marches and rallies to bring attention to this universal scourge. That sounds commendable, but it is actually in vain. See, bullying has been around since the first one-room schoolhouse was built and it will be around when all schoolhouses are converted to domiciles for invalid sportswriters and education is relegated exclusively to home computers. That's because there has always been and always will be bullies.

When we were kids in the 7th grade, the bane of our pitiful existence was a guy named Bruno who was supposed to be in the 9th grade. His name was as sinister as he was. He reminded me of a small New York mobster. My friends and I, a group of neighborhood kids whose main simple, innocuous interest was the outdoors, were the primary target of his torture. We loved to fish, hunt, camp, explore and just wanted to be left alone.

Bruno was a head taller and 40 pounds heavier than the largest of my crowd. He picked on us because he could. Simple as that. And we're talking real bullying, not the "verbal abuse" they try to pass off as bullying today. In those days, it was common to hear comments like "I'm so glad you're alive. I'm not the dumbest person in school". Or, "If I were as ugly as you, I would go home and cut my face off". Or, "Did your Mom bring you to school on her broom this morning?" And that's the stuff we said to our friends.

Hurting someone's feelings or casting doubt on their self image seems to be a major concern of the contemporary educators who hand out participation trophies. That's not bullying. Bullying is when Bruno would catch you with a surprise roundhouse fist in the middle of your back as you walked down the hall to your first period class. And you couldn't catch your breath until third period. Or when he waited until you opened your locker and in one fell swoop dumped its entire contents onto the hall floor.

Or when he grabbed you by the front and back of your jeans and gave you a life-altering wedgie. Ducky Jones wasn't the victim of this particular incivility very often. Since he spoke in a voice one or two octaves higher than most everyone, Bruno assumed some other bully had already visited that excruciatingly painful violence upon him. But the rest of us got it regularly.

One day after school, on the way to fish a creek down near The Canyon, as we affectionately dubbed the gravel pit near our neighborhood, the five or six of us were walking along complaining about Bruno when we discovered what was obviously an old Indian trail and were keeping an eye out for discarded moccasins, feather headdresses and tomahawks. We figured the place was probably heavily populated with Indians 60 or 70 years ago. (We didn't exactly have a working knowledge of archaeology or even history for that matter.)

Anyway, as we walked along said trail, we came across an outcropping of rock that literally glistened with gold. Most of us became frenetic with excitement, until Leon, the intellectual giant of our group, lackadaisically pointed out that it was iron pyrite. We were rich one moment and the next moment we went stupid. "What's iron pyrite?" one crestfallen member asked. "Fool's gold", snorted Leon, as if he were talking to one. "Oh yeah", we almost said in unison, remembering a recent Lone Ranger episode in which that particular mineral had played a part in catching the bad guys.

But in a rare stroke of juvenile genius, someone said, "I know how we can get even with Bruno" and our lives forever changed. We all sat cross-legged in an Indian circle, made a general plan and then refined it down to the smallest detail. We got a long rope, purloined from Ricky's Dad's garage, fashioned a cinch knot as a snare on one end, ran the remaining rope to the base of a large sweet gum tree growing by the iron pyrite outcrop, covered the exposed rope with leaves and ran the rest of the rope up the tree and draped it over a heavy limb.

Bobby and Bubblehead, being the heftiest of our gang, would hide in the tree holding the end of the rope and when Bruno stepped into the snare, our big boys would jump and the trap would be sprung. Foolproof. The next day, Ducky and Leon and Ricky and I approached Bruno at school and told him of our gold find, showed him a small paper sack full of the stuff and asked him to accompany us to retrieve the mother load. A suspicious and inevitable "Why me?" question came up and Leon explained that he was the biggest and baddest guy we knew and we would feel safe knowing no one would try to steal it from us if he came along. Flattery and greed ruled the day.

After school, we let Bobby and Bubblehead get a head start to hide in the tree and we brought Bruno along shortly thereafter. When we got to the gold, I told Bruno to "stand right there" so he could see both up and down the trail while we pulled the gold out and stuffed our pockets. As soon as he stepped into the camouflaged snare, Bobby and Bubblehead jumped from the sweet gum, rope tightly in hand.

I can't describe the speed with which Bruno was snatched upside down and into the air about 4 feet off the ground. You had to be there. He was caught on his right leg just below the knee and was flailing helplessly about and flapping his arms like a wounded penguin while Bobby and Bubblehead held on tight. Looking back, I don't know how it didn't break his leg or dislocate his hip, but God even looks out after bullies.

We let him hang there and screech and curse and threaten for a full five minutes. That slowly turned to begging and when he began blubbering and calling for mommy, we let him down. With an admonition. If he ever even approached us again, we would relate this incident to everyone in school. With great embellishments.

And this, folks, is the way to prevent bullying. Of course, many will disagree with it, calling it inhumane and hurtful to fragile psyches. But those people aren't looking for solutions. They just want to create perpetual victims who will be their allies in their next agenda, whatever in God's name that may be at the time. As for me, I know our resolution worked. Bruno never bothered any of us again.

Chapter Twelve

LESSONS LEARNED AT THE STATE FAIR

When I was a kid and the mornings in September began to dawn cooler and crisper, anticipation always grew because everyone knew the State Fair was on the way. But when I was 12 or so, the expectation became particularly sharp because the rumor spread amongst us neighborhood kids that among the prizes at the game booths that year were Zebco 33's and Black Lightning rods! Each of my gang of buddies saved every penny we could get our hands on. Allowances were hoarded. We canvassed the neighborhood relentlessly in search of yard work. Paper route collection day took on an air of bookies demanding payment from tardy losers.

Fortunately, the fairgrounds were located right across the road from us. On the long awaited appointed night, six or so of us gathered at Ducky's house and trekked the three or four blocks to the State Fair. I would not travel that particular route today with a squad of armed Navy Seals, but back then, it was safe and harmless. We were jocular, our pockets bulging with coin and our spirits high.

When we hit the sawdust and woodchip midway, the cacophony of sounds smells and sights were almost overwhelming. It was difficult to concentrate on our goal of discovering which booth had the coveted rods and reels we sought. Between the games were rides operated by scruffy men with bottles of rye whisky in their back pockets. They looked like they hadn't slept in 3 days and smelled like they hadn't bathed in a week. That odor mixed with the burnt popcorn and the droppings in the pony rides was almost a deadly combination. But we focused on our quest.

We began to get a little desperate as we neared the end of the first side of the oval midway and had not seen any displayed prizes but stuffed animals and kewpie dolls. Of course, we were hampered by Bubblehead and Bobby. Bubblehead simply could not pass by any cotton candy vendor without buying a stick of the stuff. After 30 minutes, he had spent most of his money and his face was fluffy with remnants of pink sugar. He looked like a garden gnome. It was embarrassing. And it takes a lot to embarrass a 12 year old.

And we had to go back and retrieve Bobby every few minutes from a sideshow. He would be standing enraptured in front of a barker announcing "Step right up ladies and gentlemen, boys and girls. See the Alligator Woman. She walks, she talks..." Then there was the Bearded Lady. "She walks, she talks..." then there was the World's Smallest Horse. That last one was sort of intriguing and we all spent one of our quarters to take a gander. On the side of the tent was a picture of a pony standing in a man's hand. We walked through the curtain to discover a card table sitting in the middle of the room. On it was an equine fetus in a jar of formaldehyde. We all feigned interest in it to one another so we wouldn't have to admit we had just wasted 25 cents. And after all, the man didn't say it walked or talked.

Halfway down the second side of the midway, we came across the goldfish booth. I had learned long ago not to waste my money on it. It looked easy at first. You stood outside the counter and pitched ping pong balls to a table full of fishbowls in hopes the ball would land inside the bowl, thereby winning a fish. Two problems. The bowls were big, but the opening in the bowl was about the size of a Mason jar lid. Also, if you happened to get really, really lucky and you actually won one, they put the unfortunate fish in a tiny plastic bag full of water, which you had to carry around until you got home, only to discover said fish had expired.

Of course, Bubblehead just had to try. He spent his last quarter and got 3 ping pong balls. His hands were so gooey from cotton candy residue he had to throw as hard as he could just to get the ball out of his grasp, which severely limited his accuracy, not that it mattered. Lo and behold, the Good Lord looks after the stupid and the sticky. There was a midway miracle that night and Bubblehead won not one, but two goldfish. He couldn't play any more games or buy anymore cotton candy because he was out of money and out of hands to hold anything but a goldfish in each one. He just glumly followed us on our rapidly deflating search.

We were almost at the end and thinking the rumor had been a hoax when someone spotted them! Among the stuffed bears and rabbits, there were three beautiful, gleaming rods and reels! They were at the "Lucky Duck" booth and the carnie was fairly screaming, "Step right up! Grab a lucky duck and win a prize. Everyone's a winner with a lucky duck!" He was looking right at us.

The premise was simple. Right on the front counter was a trough with continuously running water that went under a cover on one end and came out at the other end. It was full of a hundred little bobbing plastic ducks. For 25 cents, you just picked one up, looked at the number on the bottom and showed it to the barker. The number corresponded with the prize you would receive. And it was true. Everyone won a prize.

But there was one small problem that did not register in our tiny little 6th grade brains. There was no sign or chart designating which number corresponded with which prize. That was o.k. though, because we were sure the guy in the booth knew them all by heart. (As if he had a heart).

Considering the name of the game, we all appointed Ducky to go first. And then we each took turns handing the guy money and picking a duck. There was a tray behind the duck tunnel that we couldn't see and each time the proprietor looked at the number, he automatically reached into that tray to produce our prize. And each prize was some 2 cent joke that came from a Cracker Jack box. You know, a plastic ring, a stick-on tattoo, a 4 piece puzzle, etc. Only one of those prizes drew any interest.

He handed someone a half-dozen clear plastic swizzle sticks wrapped in a rubber band. Now, we didn't know what a swizzle stick was, but upon closer inspection, we discovered that the handle of the stick was the silhouette of a naked lady and that was the best prize we had won so far. Everybody took one. After that, it was back to the cheap stuff. Not once did the guy ever even turn and make a step to the rear where the rods and reels and stuffed animals were.

I was already thinking this must be some kind of hustle my Dad had warned me about and I had promptly ignored. With my last quarter, I picked up duck #14, and having drawn it before, expected another tiny rubber pig. But the guy handed me a cheap pen instead. The little hamster wheel in my head where my brain was supposed to be began to turn. I immediately responded to his con game with a scathing verbal retort. I said, "Heyyyyyy". He knew the jig was up. "Sorry kids, gotta close. Come back tomorrow night." He shut off the booth light and disappeared.

We shuffled home that night with a lot less enthusiasm than we had begun the evening. Bubblehead stopped and emptied his dead goldfish into a storm drain and mumbled a short eulogy. He had already named them. Nothing much else was said. We were all a bit smarter. The only real laugh we got out of the trip was the next day when Bobby told us his mother had found his swizzle stick in his jeans pocket and had beaten the crap out of him.

The next time I went to the State Fair, I was in college. I finally got to see the Alligator Woman. It was a girl with psoriasis in a one piece bathing suit. And the Bearded Lady was a guy in a dress. As I walked the midway, reminiscing, I came across the Lucky Duck game booth. In the menagerie of stuffed animals, there sat three Zebco reels and Black Lightning rods. I gave the guy 50 cents (inflation) and picked up a plastic duck. Number 14. I grinned, took my stick of gum and went home.

P.T. Barnum said there was a sucker born every minute. I say, for every sucker, there is a wise man waiting to get out.

Chapter Thirteen

SNOW DAYS

School snow days for kids in the Deep South are as rare as magazine sweepstakes winners. You are probably familiar with the concept. The magazine folks bring a giant $1,000,000 cardboard check to people's doors with TV cameras in tow, obviously hoping that the shock will cause the recipient to fall over dead so no money will actually change hands.

Anyway, when I was a kid, we only had two snow days during twelve years of school. I went fishing on one occasion and hunting on the other and learned a great deal both times. But not about hunting and fishing.

When I was 12 or 13, the temperature dropped to like eleventy something below freezing and we had what we assumed was a blizzard one night because there was an entire inch of the strange and magical white stuff on the ground the next morning. School was gloriously called off.

When Ducky awoke that morning, he discovered his little brother's plastic pool was frozen solid. He ran excitedly to my house, surprisingly without snowshoes, and breathlessly exclaimed we had to go ice-fishing down at the strip mine pit.

Now, we had read about and seen pictures of ice-fishing, had always wanted to try it, and this was literally the opportunity of a lifetime. We grabbed our spin casting rods, a few crappie jigs, a hatchet with which to cut a hole in the ice and took off walking to the pond. We marveled at the crunch of the snow under our stupid little feet.

The pit was one huge sheet of glistening ice. With a lapse in judgment of Biblical proportions, we decided to go out to the middle to cut our hole. We gingerly walked, slid and slipped approximately 5 feet from the bank before said ice cracked, gave way and left us both standing knee deep in breathtaking, mind-numbing ice water.

Lesson #1: Ice is always thickest near the bank. Lesson #2: The thermal qualities of a wading pool are not those of a 30 foot deep lake. Lesson #3: Walking home through the snow in wet tennis shoes is a painful and humbling experience. Especially with no fish.

When it snowed again only a few years later, we conjectured a new ice age was upon us. Snow had been forecast a few days before the actual event, and in spite of the prognostications of my Great Aunt Mary, I was looking forward to it. She had told me it was too cold to snow. Whaaaat? That was like saying it was too cloudy to rain. Of course, she had told my folks that she hadn't been worried about the last tornado warning we had because, and I quote, "The river would cut it off". I was actually related to this person. She lived in a little town called Sycamore and I am convinced that she was single-handedly responsible for the inhabitants of that little hamlet being referred to as "Sycamorons".

Anyway, Ducky and I were in high school when the second snow of our lifetime occurred. We grabbed our .22's, jumped in his beat up 1940 something pickup truck and headed to the country for some small game hunting. There had been ice on the road, but it was mid-morning and sunny and it had all disappeared. Except. When we reached to top of a rather steep hill, we hadn't realized the downhill side was a western slope and the sun had not touched it. It was slicker than a lifelong politician. The Olympics could have held a bob-sledding competition for the next half mile.

As soon as we hit it, the old truck began to slide and Ducky slammed on brakes. Now, even in the South, everyone knows you don't touch the brakes on an icy road. But we weren't everyone. We were teenagers. The most ignorant form of life on earth. Fortunately, no one else was on that stretch of rural road, so we had full use of both lanes. And we needed them.

So began Ducky's sit-down comedy act with the steering wheel. At times, he held it steady in a death grip. At other times he was spinning it wildly back and forth with absolute abandon. Apparently, there was no rhyme or reason for his choice of direction except possible animal instinct. And the whole time, he kept the brakes jammed to the floor as we gained speed. I, of course, was giving him calm and perfectly logical instructions. Between screams. They consisted of such management commands as "turn right! Right! No, left! Turn left! Put on braaaaaaaaakes!" And so forth.

For a half mile, we slid, gaining momentum the entire time. I know we turned completely around twice and at one point were facing backward for a while, staring in wide-eyed wonderment at where we had been. Most of the time, we were sideways. I do remember thinking, this was a slow and cruel way to die, because you actually had time to contemplate how it might happen and how excruciatingly painful it was going to be.

Somehow, we never left the road and when it opened into sunlight again and the pavement was dry, we were facing the right way and in our own lane. After we slid to a stop (Ducky still had the brake on), we sat there a moment, silently gazing out the windshield. Ducky said, "Well. That was interesting." He always had a knack for understatement. I replied, "I have to go to the bathroom". Ducky said, "I've already been".

After a thankfully uneventful half hour, we reached our hunting ground. I mentioned earlier that I had learned something on both snow days. On this one, I discovered you can actually divine someone's personality by the way they interpret tracks in the snow.

We were trailing a fox in an old corn field when its tracks intercepted those of a quail. There were a bunch of feathers and some blood in the snow. The fox tracks continued on into the woods and there were no more bird tracks to be seen. I said to Ducky, "Well, it's pretty obvious what happened here". He replied, "It sure is. That quail must have jumped on Mr. Fox's back, pecked his head 'til it was bloody and then flew off". I just stared at him for a moment. "Okaaaaaaaay".

It dawned on me then that Ducky was an unrepentant champion of the underdog. And observing him over a lifetime has proven me correct. Perhaps it is because Ducky himself is a perpetual underdog. And as such, it would only be poetic justice if he were to win that magazine sweepstakes one of these days. I just hope they don't scare him to death.

Chapter Fourteen

THE DAM RIVER RATS

I remember the year my friends and I were in the 8th grade with great clarity. And horror. That was the year we regularly fished the river below Jordan Dam on the weekends. Of course, we had no way to get there, but there was a guy in the neighborhood named Mac who was a few years older than us and he had a driver's license. Now, high schoolers and junior high schoolers didn't normally hang out together because that was just, well, wrong. It was an unwritten social code.

But there are times that nature allows species to coexist for mutual benefit. Both we and Mac loved to fish. Mac had a car and dated girls, so he was always broke. We had lawn cutting and paper route money and nothing much to spend it on. He provided the transportation and we provided the gas. Mutual benefit.

Now, when I say Mac had a "car", I use the word reluctantly. It was more akin to an unarmed tank. If you've never seen a 1950 Nash Metropolitan, look it up on the internet. You're in for a treat. It resembles a giant turtle and is completely devoid of any aesthetic qualities whatsoever. The only way it could have been any uglier is if it was painted lime green. Mac's was painted lime green. How he ever got a girl to get in that thing is beyond my powers of comprehension.

However, for transporting kids to the river, it was perfect. Mac had somewhat customized his vehicle. He had removed the back seat and the partition to the trunk, installed half-inch plywood and upholstered it with soft seat cover material. In retrospect, that project obviously had something to do with dating girls. At the time however, we couldn't imagine why he did that, but we loved it. Since

Mac was short for his age, he drove with the front seat all the way up and there was an enormous amount of room in the back.

It could have slept 8 adults or 16 kids comfortably. On the way to the dam, Mac practiced a little trick that was singular with the old Nash. He would jerk the steering wheel a half-turn and immediately release it. On its own, the car would go into a swaying motion for a couple of hundred yards until it corrected itself. I don't think that was an intentional safety feature of the vehicle, but I could be wrong. To six kids in the back, it was like a ride at the state fair. We would tumble and roll from one side to the other, completely helpless, laughing and giggling all the while.

It wasn't really as dangerous as it sounds. The thing had to weigh about 6 tons, and even if it had rolled over, we would have been relatively safe. I saw one hit a city dump truck head on once. The grill of the truck was completely destroyed and both front tires flattened. The Metropolitan suffered a scratch on one headlight cover.

One Saturday, we rock and rolled our way up to the river. That was the day we came up with a name for ourselves: The Dam River Rats. It was perfect. It smacked of renegades, bravado and reckless obscenity, yet we couldn't be accused of cursing. Our maturity and intellect were something to behold.

When we got there that fateful day, there was only one gate open on the dam and the river was barely 50 yards across. It was about 300 yards to the riverbed from the parking area at the top and the first half of that was just a few degrees off of perfectly vertical. It was unseasonably hot that day and we actually broke into a sweat climbing down.

That was surprising, because I don't think kids had sweat glands in those days. We had been raised in the Deep South without air conditioners. Most of us didn't even have a window fan in the house. So no one perspired until you started dating or filled out your first W-2 form. By the time we negotiated what was laughingly referred to as a trail down that cliff, desperately clinging to the kudzu to keep from plunging to certain death, we were soaking wet. Someone in our little group later told me that gave them an ominous premonition. I don't know. Kids lie a lot.

But it felt good to get to the relative cool of the rocks and boulders which comprised the second half of our journey sloping down to the water. We walked and climbed our way down to a residual pool of about a half acre directly on the face of the dam. Standing there looking up at that huge structure was truly awesome.

It was the largest man-made edifice any of us had ever seen at the time. We felt how Dorothy must have looking up and the throne of Oz. And there was the roar of the rushing water to our right and the mind-numbing buzz of the generators inside the structure. It was almost a religious experience. The pool was chock full of big blue cats and we baited with minnows or worms and began pulling them in every other cast. There were a couple of paddlefish trapped in there and someone hung one and it promptly broke his line. Like I say, it was almost heaven. Until the warning horn blew.

The sound was quite unmistakable as it could be heard 8 miles downstream and rendered anyone in the immediate vicinity temporarily stone deaf. It meant the gates would be opening in 10 minutes and we had to quit fishing and head for high ground. Quickly. But this day, either the engineer had suffered a stroke or had forgotten how to tell time or the Great and Powerful Oz was playing with us. Before we even had a chance to reel in, the quiet pool in which we were fishing became a violent maelstrom. A veritable tidal wave from 4 open gates hit each of us at the knees or waist, according to our height.

Bait, minnow buckets, two stringers of catfish, all gone. In unspeakable panic, rods and reels were either dropped or actually thrown, perhaps in hopes of appeasing the river gods. We were like ants in a bathtub. Though hysterical to the point of insanity, we still had enough sense or primordial instinct to head up the slope.

I glanced around and saw everyone's eyes were bugged out like cartoon characters, but were blind with pure terror. Mac, by far the oldest and most wise of us, screamed, "We're all gonna dieeeeeeee!" so you can imagine the state of mind (and I use that term loosely) the rest of us were in. Personally, I never doubted Mac for a moment.

Now, if you aren't familiar with them, river rocks have a peculiar attribute. When they are dry, they have a flaky film that actually serve as an adhesive and are easy to walk on. When a drop of water touches them however, they become as slick as an eel dipped in Crisco. So in our quest to achieve the kudzu cliff before the rising water, we waded, fell, climbed, fell, stood, fell, sloshed, fell, splashed, fell, gurgled, fell, swam, and, rose and fell again. That's when lightning hit a transformer on the dam.

Mac repeated his admonition, "We're all gonna dieeeeeee!" What Mac lacked in stature, he made up for in volume. It was at that point that I gave up all hope of survival. I think I simply dismissed reality as something I could not deal with at the time because I distinctly remember being concerned that my wallet was wet. Now, a 13 year old has no more need of a wallet than an old man has of track shoes. All that was in mine was my lucky $2 bill (which was not working at the time), a folded-up really bad report card that never made it home and a school picture of the ugliest girl in my math class.

This particular young lady had the habit of writing notes to me every day. You know the kind. "I like you. Do you like me? Yes or No. Mark the square." I never answered, but was happy to have the distraction. Anything was better than math. And once, she passed said picture in one of the notes. I could not understand why the most unattractive member of the opposite sex was interested in me. It never occurred to me that water seeks its own level.

Speaking of which, we somehow managed to reach the kudzu at the high water mark and clung breathlessly to it, skinned, bruised and battered, sincerely surprised to be alive. It was still lightning, but we were out of the water. It became apparent that the storm, which we couldn't see coming because the dam was in the way, had roared down the lake, dumping untold tons of water and causing the dam personnel to open the gates so abruptly.

With sudden courage, borne of new found safety, someone scoffed at Mac, "I thought we were all gonna die". Though Mac's prognostication had been incorrect, he was still smarter than the rest of us. He simply replied, "You wanna walk home?" No one else chose to say anything.

We never went to the river after that trip and the Dam River Rats disbanded. We did found another organization though. The Dang BB Bangers. But that's another story.

Chapter Fifteen

THE DANG BB BANGERS

When I was 13 years old, my neighborhood friends and I formed a hunting club. It seemed like the right thing to do at the time. Don't ask me where we came up with the name. We were 13.

That was the age at which my mother would ask me a cryptic question at least once a week when I got up in the morning. "How old are you today?" I never understood at the time. Though the question was obviously rhetorical, it often startled me into thinking I had forgotten my birthday. But I did not realize that a young teenager's feelings, emotions, intellect and actions fluctuated on a daily basis to place you anywhere between the ages of 8 and 21 at any given time and my mother's question was in reality beyond my grasp. Hence, "The Dang BB Bangers" came from the collective deeply cerebral minds of 13 year olds.

The goal of our hunting club was to rid the world of blackbirds. Much like farmers tried to do with crows. And for pretty much the same reasons. The farmers protected corn. We protected vegetable gardens. Everybody had them in those days. And we young men had to plant, hoe, weed and water those gardens. In effect, we were insuring that our hard work didn't go to waste.

Having blackbirds eating from the garden you meticulously tended was like having spent hours writing some stupid theme for English class and having Ducky Jones get a hold of it and erase every other word on the paper. And you didn't know it and turned it in that way. If only I had had a BB gun in my hands then.

Anyway, we couldn't shoot songbirds. Mom said so, Dad said so, preacher said so and teacher said so. It was a sin to shoot a songbird. But none of the many subspecies of blackbirds (starling, grackle, redwing, cowbird, etc.) had singing ability so they were fair game. The vocalizations of robins, mockingbirds, and cardinals saved them, much the same as some Hollywood celebrities today.

We never shot each other. Not that it would have been all that painful. If you've ever been peppered with a load of #8's from across a dove field, a BB from 20 feet isn't much worse. And a slingshot-launched chinaberry is much more devastating. But we refrained from such attacks because we knew the victim wouldn't retaliate in kind. It would be more likely that he would grab the weapon by the barrel and take to your head like a bar biker with a pool cue. And no one wanted that.

We harvested a surprising amount of blackbirds the first week or so of our quest. And we knew good hunters always ate their quarry, so we cleaned a few and roasted them on someone's open pit barbeque grill. Quail are delicious. Dove are passing fair. Blackbirds are edible — if you have been chained to a dungeon wall and starved for a week. We took to giving them to the neighborhood cats.

We became so proficient at taking blackbirds that someone suggested we go for big game. So late one afternoon, we jumped on our bikes and headed for the city dump to try our hand at rats, which were more than plentiful. We discovered that a BB not only wouldn't kill them, it just pissed them off. Real bad. Now, we're not talking field mice here. Some of these things were as large as small hogs. One or two would actually make a false charge after they were hit. I swear a couple of them screamed at us. Once, little Ricky dropped his rifle and ran like a French soldier at Moscow. From then on, we stuck with blackbirds.

Like most life-altering decisions men make, women were at the center of my resolution to leave The Dang BB Bangers. One day after school, I grabbed my J.C. Higgins lever action and stalked to the edge of my house to scout for the black garden raiders. Two girls from my class were walking by in the street and watching me. I had only recently begun to have a strange (and delightful) attraction to the opposite sex, and this was a perfect opportunity to impress them.

I spotted a partially obscured blackbird in the nearest row of peas, took careful aim and squeezed off a perfect head shot. Turns out, not only was it not a blackbird, but I had wounded it in such a way that it grotesquely tumbled head over heels across the yard, screeching piteously all the way. The girls stopped in horror and screamed, "He shot a robin! He shot a robin!" in a tone and manner that proclaimed I had murdered and beheaded my mother.

The Junior High School grapevine is swift and vicious. The next day, as I walked down the hall, every girl in school had excommunicated me from humanity and would say, "ewwwww" and turn away from me as I passed. Occasionally, some guy would whisper "Nice shot" when he walked by. It was then that I decided if I wanted a date to next year's Junior High Prom, I would have to resign from the Bangers.

So, I hung up my BB gun, waited another year until I got a .22 and could go into the deep woods and hunt squirrels, away from the prying eyes of females. Such is life.

Chapter Sixteen

BIKER BOYS

When I was a kid, shortly after the last Ice Age, our bicycles served as our ATV's and four-wheelers. Then a magical thing happened when we turned 14. We could ride motorcycles less than 200 cc's with a special license. Five of us neighborhood kids immediately gave up our bicycles on our birthdays and talked our Dads into coming off of 50 to 75 bucks for a little used Harley. The cost would be supplemented by our paper route and lawn cutting money. I told my Dad I would never, ever, ask for a car when I turned 16 if only I could have a motorcycle at 14. He asked if I would be willing to wait until I was 21. I thought he had lost his mind. "Of course!"

The little Harleys were only slightly faster than a well-pedaled bicycle, but we could go a lot further on them and we never got tired. Gas in those days was only a little more expensive than the price of air and we got something like 2,000 miles per gallon. They were our tickets to the Great Outdoors!

Of course, we didn't just take them fishing and hunting. We went everywhere on them. School, movies, the skating rink, girl's houses, etc. We thought we were pretty cool, but actually riding a motorcycle wasn't all that great. Oh, there were a few exciting times. A bee flew in my mouth once. We were both terribly surprised. For you younger enthusiasts out there, if a stinging insect flies into your mouth at 30mph, do not (a) let go of the handlebars or (b) close your mouth.

And once, I waved to my girlfriend's father as I cruised past their house, which was situated on a hairpin curve. In those days my grasp of fundamental physics — velocity times distance divided by arc and curb height plus bike weight squared by rose bush — was not what it is today. I recall regaining consciousness with Nancy's father slapping me (rather viciously in retrospect) and saying "Son, are you alright?" And I remember sitting up and wondering why his neighbors would plow up their lawn in the middle of the summer and tear down all those beautiful flowers.

My four buddies and I rode to Junior High together each morning. We would pull into the school yard in unison, hoping to attract attention. But the little 100's and 125's just didn't roar like the big bikes some of the older teenagers had. They just hummed. Softly. Like a small swarm of houseflies.

I dreamed that some day we would glide into the parking lot in a Blue Angel formation and the girls would stop dead in their tracks, stare in awe and smile in admiration. That never happened. Sometimes, though, one would point and giggle.

You had to be careful with whom you rode. In those days, there were no laws requiring helmets and the more radical bikers had a lot of wrecks. You could easily spot them. They sat through green lights, revving their engines. They tended to wear headbands, ostensibly to cover the nuts and bolts with which their skulls were repaired. If you spoke to one, they would say things like, "Hey man, am I facing the right way?" Our little group of outdoorsmen stayed away from them.

Going out on a date was somewhat of a drawback. My girlfriend Nancy's father, having witnessed the singular mishap I mentioned earlier, was, you might say, somewhat apprehensive about letting her ride on the back of my Harley. As a matter of fact, I recall he forbade her to even go near it and advised that, should she touch it, she would turn into a pillar of salt. And I think he mentioned something about a convent.

Our little motorcycles just weren't girl-getters. In truly cold weather, between the wind and the tears streaking around to the back of your head, a hairstyle known as the "ducktail" was born. And sometimes, your lips would freeze. It was truly invigorating, but it was not a good idea to meet a girl after a cold weather ride.

"Garry", a friend once said, "I would like you to meet Monica. She is going to be Junior High head cheerleader next year." "Mmmmmmmmphhhhh", I replied. "Pleaff ta mendja". "You ride a motorcycle don't you?" she questioned in a tone reminiscent of asking if you ate your young. "Nuh uh, nuh uh. Demtis. Wem ta demtis!" "You haven't been to the dentist", she sneered. "I can see your ducktail!"

She, like most other girls, wanted a man with a car. I struck out in both categories. Anyway, I had Nancy. True, her father was a little to the political right of Attila the Hun and wouldn't let her leave the house with me, but on the other hand, I didn't know what to do on a date anyway.

Despite the drawbacks, our little motorcycles more than made up for their social shortcomings as the key to outdoor heaven. I have yet to see a modern ATV go anywhere we couldn't go. We would put our two-piece spin casting outfits and bait in our saddlebags and off to the wilderness we would go. One of our favorite fishing holes was an oxbow lake down by the river. It was located on Farmer Brown's (no kidding) place and he charged a dollar to fish on his property. Now, a dollar would fill up the gas tanks on our little Harley's twice, so naturally we were somewhat reluctant to pay that much for the privilege to fish.

The entrance to his farm was downhill, so very early in the morning, we would approach the farmhouse, cut our engines and coast past. When we judged we were out of earshot, we would drop into second gear, pop the clutch and be on our way. I know, I know. But we weren't bad kids. We were just kids. Juvenile delinquents, in those days, were guys who stole hubcaps and sold them to the local junkyard. We didn't make any money from our sinful deed, we were just trying to save some. Besides, looking back, I am sure Farmer Brown was probably looking out his kitchen window, coffee cup in hand, and saying to his wife, "Look at those little fools. They'll probably grow up to be lawyers".

On the swampy off-road trail we had made from one end of the lake to the other, we rode in single file. When the guy up front yelled, "Snake!" we would lift our legs and gun the bikes. We left a lot of pissed-off reptiles on that trail. Once though, our leader yelled "Gator!" and there was a huge pile up. It was terrifying. If I had lived long enough at that time to have actually qualified as having a life, I'm sure it would have flashed before my eyes. I did have a short sequential montage of Mom beating the crap out of me for various offenses, but that probably did not meet the conditions of a near-death experience flashback. After a lot of cursing, confusion, hopping up and down in place and frantically searching around for a snarling, leviathan we determined we were not going to be eaten alive. We unbent our fenders and crash bars and went on our way.

We took our bikes on some fine squirrel hunting trips. We would stick the butts of our .22's and .410's in the saddle bags, strap them down with the barrels pointing rearward and head to the woods. That specific mode of transporting our firearms probably made the occasional driver behind us on the highway a bit nervous, but most people paid no attention. There were no terrorists or school shootings or drive-by's back then. The police even ignored us most of the time.

Once, however, on our way back to town, a highway patrolman pulled us over. The five of us sat on the edge of the road and the trooper walked straight up to Ducky Jones. Over the course of the season, Ducky had tied squirrel tails to every conceivable place on his bike to which one could be tied. When moving, his motorcycle looked like a large crytozoological mammal trying to become airborne. The officer was eyeing the tag and tail light which were obscured by the furry things.

Now, Ducky had an excessive, irrational fear of authority figures, so when the officer asked him for his license, Ducky lost all control of his bodily functions. Such was the thunderous sound that emitted from Ducky, the cop actually jumped back, probably expecting him to explode. And when the stench hit, the man wheeled and walked off to his patrol car, with the passing admonition, "You boys be careful". It has always been my philosophy that abject fear is not necessarily a bad thing.

I will never forget our motorcycling adventures. The fact that your hands sometimes froze to the handlebar grips or that raindrops felt like shotgun pellets or that cars seemed forever intent on running you over, didn't matter. We had the freedom of the outdoors. And nothing was more important than that. Not even girls.

Chapter Seventeen

PHOBIA

Fear is not necessarily a bad thing. I have a theory that the accumulative effects of fear build character and since outdoorsmen are more likely to encounter danger than other people, we are emotionally stronger, intellectually wiser and more physically intrepid than your average citizen. I myself have so many fears as to be almost superhuman. I am deathly afraid of snakes, regardless of size or species. I am afraid of being in the deep woods and meeting two men with straw hats, shotguns and five teeth between them who say, "Hey, boy. Anybody know yore out heah?". I am afraid of unmarked electrified fences, rusty tree stands, cross-eyed firearms instructors, deranged pigs and any ammo I have personally reloaded.

I learned at a young age that personal abject terror is not the only aspect of fear. Understanding its nuances, I was able to appreciate the humor of fear in others. And the fact that even that can come back to bite you in the butt. Case in point. A half-dozen or so of us preteen kids in my neighborhood used to sneak into the back nine of the local golf course and fish the water hazards there.

It was usually pretty good fishing, but we sometimes had to contend with the guardian of the country club, Willie the groundskeeper. He was a terrifying old man who often carried a gnarled Scottish walking stick. If he were strolling on foot down the fairways, he would spot us, yell, wield the stick above his head like a sword and give chase while we scattered to the four winds.

One particular afternoon, he was almost upon us before we realized it and we broke like a covey of quail. I chose to run to a storage shed by #9 tee box. There I hid in the front corner of the structure and held my breath, expecting him to enter any second and beat me to death. To my surprise, Ducky Jones, 30 seconds behind me but apparently having an amount of strategic intelligence equal to my own, decided to hide in that self-same shed. Unfortunately for Ducky, he lacked the forethought to look where he was going and backed into the corner I already occupied.

My initial fear now turned to anticipation. And to make it even more enjoyable, he was creeping ever so slowly backward, keeping an eye out the door for Willie. I had time to consider many possibilities. Touch him on the shoulder. Snatch his cap off. Grab him and yell "Gotcha!" I opted for the low growl. It took him several milliseconds to react.

First, he inhaled so much air, I thought the entire building would implode. Then, almost in slow motion, his arms began to flail and his feet began to dance. But he didn't go anywhere and he didn't look back. Obviously, he did not want to see what was about to eat him and he didn't want to flee and provoke an attack. He just sort of hung there, as if in midair, like a gigantic, psychotic puppet, limbs jerking helplessly. I was gleeful.

The resounding screech I expected never came. He just kept inhaling and then all movement ceased and he collapsed in a little pile. He was completely still. And he smelled bad. Now, fear once again turned its ugly head to me. My mind raced. "Mr. Jones, he was running from Willie the groundskeeper. He must have died from exhaustion." Or, "Honest Mrs. Jones, I think there were rabid bats in that shed. He must have died from bat bites." Or, "It must have been fumes from the fertilizer, Your Honor." Fortunately, Ducky regained consciousness and beat the crap out of me. Boy, was I relieved.

There was another configuration of fear that I learned in my mid-teens. Fear can be your friend. I was at that awkward age when boys really like girls, but are scared to death of them. I was at the final weigh-in of a bass tournament where several family members were in contention to win. My brother Marvin was there also. He is several years my senior and was the bane of adolescents everywhere.

He happened to be with his girlfriend and her drop-dead gorgeous younger sister. He walked up out of nowhere and said nothing but, "Garry, this is Starr", wheeled around, girlfriend on his arm, and walked away, chuckling. I had always thought my parents adopted him from a troupe of circus clowns.

Starr said, "Hi".

I said, "Bliffet".

She said, "Pardon?"

I said, "Bliffet. Mitch boggling framer docklet".

She said, "Oh, I just love foreign languages".

I said, "Minnow loggem".

She said, "Wanna go get a hotdog?"

I said, "Clatcher".

I never did find out who won the tournament. But it was a wonderful evening. It even ended with a goodnight marfal.

Fear is nothing to be afraid of. Embrace it. It won't let you down.

Chapter Eighteen

GUNS 'N RODS 'N ROSES

People who look back on their high school days as the greatest time of their life are the same people who say, "No officer, I don't have a license. I just got out of prison yesterday". When we were 16, we were stupid, maladroit, and completely devoid of social skills. High school was a place to go between hunting and fishing trips in order to meet girls. Consequently, our romantic interests and love of the outdoors became inextricably intertwined.

That is how one Spring weekend afternoon found Ducky Jones and I headed to a little meadow by a pond we frequently fished. We had two young ladies in tow for a picnic and possible dalliance. We unloaded the basket of food and blankets and walked down the short trail to the pond. As we rounded a bend, there was the largest timber rattler I had ever seen coiled in the middle of the path. It was as thick as a fire hose and its rattles sounded like a skill saw.

Now, those of you who share my deep, almost psychotic, aversion to snakes will understand when I say the very sight of it almost made me physically ill. You know who you are. My date spotted it at the same time I did, squealed, and jumped into my arms. For a second,

I was transformed from a gangly, ignorant teenager into a masculine manly-man rescuing a damsel in distress. For a second.

I don't know if I had been rendered powerless by the mere sight of that revolting leviathan or if my date was a tad overweight, but my arms gave way and my knees buckled and I unceremoniously dropped her on the spot. Not only that, but my bladder, completely independent of any conscious thought, chose that moment to void itself. And when the girl on the ground in front of me looked up with widening eyes, the first thing she saw was my slowly darkening jeans, mere inches from her face.

She said some words I didn't know girls knew, struggled to her feet with purpose and determination and strode back up the trail towards the car. The picnic seemed to be over. Any notion of getting lucky quickly evaporated, unlike the front of my jeans, which Ducky was happy to point out on our walk back. Several times.

That same year, a friend of a friend invited Ducky and I to his house on a Saturday night to meet a writer for a national outdoor magazine, who was a friend of his parents. That was intriguing in itself, as there was the possibility we could regale him with tales of our outdoor prowess which might end up in print. But the friend had also assured us there would be girls there. It was a no-brainer. Which, incidentally, perfectly described me.

What we walked into was a party of 40 year old adults in full inebriated swing. The first thing I did was knock over a lamp as I tried to close the door behind me. The second thing I did was try to catch the lamp, which resulted in three wine glasses and a large ashtray becoming airborne. Somewhere in the middle of this Chevy Chase dance, I stepped on the cat. The only thing that drowned out the poor animal's screeches was the raucous guffaws of the revelers, every one of which was looking at me.

Since the door was still open, the cat and I left. Years afterward, strangers would walk up to me and say, "Heyyyy, weren't you the guy that…" "No!" I would interrupt. "I wasn't there!"

My senior year, I had a steady girlfriend with which I was getting nowhere, romantically. I came up with a devious plan, brought into existence entirely by teenage hormones, and took her to the firing range with my 12 gauge. I showed her the proper grip and stance and she dry fired it a few times. Then I loaded it up with high brass double oughts and let her fire for real. When I helped her up off the ground, I told her I needed to take off her blouse so I could check her for deep bruising.

She couldn't use her right arm, but she slapped me with her left hand so hard it loosened a filling. Teenaged girls are a lot smarter than teenaged boys, but that's not saying much. So are most small game animals.

A couple of weeks before our Senior Prom, I still did not have a date. Every girl I asked said "No" in varying degrees of emphasis. The best declinations were simply, "Sorry, but I already have a date". The worst were a string of expletives followed by hysterical laughter. So, I fell back on my knowledge of the outdoors.

Baiting deer was illegal at the time, but I instinctively knew it would work or it wouldn't be illegal. So I started a rumor that my rich Uncle had passed away and I was going to be fabulously wealthy. I gave the gossip time to gestate and circulate and tried again. This time, I went for the 200 yard head shot with iron sights and asked a cheerleader to the Big Dance. For those of you not familiar with the hierarchy of high school social order, asking a cheerleader out was tantamount to requesting an audience with the British Queen.

She fluttered her eyelashes and asked, "What kind of car will you be picking me up in?" This girl was not only oblivious to ending a sentence in a preposition, but totally unaware that her motives were so transparent. Look up "gold-digger" in the dictionary. That's her picture next to it. But I had asked for it.

I blurted out, "A '57 Nash Rambler."

Astonished, she said, "Ewwwwww! I heard you were rich!"

Utilizing one of the very few things I learned in two years of Civics classes, I pleaded, "Not until the will is probated." (I was actually surprised that fell out of my mouth.)

She said, "Call me when it is," turned on her heel and sashayed away, never to speak to me again.

So, I fell back on another sports strategy. When the bass aren't biting, fish for carp. I began approaching the buck-toothed, bow-legged and befuddled. By the way, they turned out to be the most beautiful, successful and well-adjusted adults, but being as dumb as deranged turtles, we didn't know that at the time. Anyway, thinking something was wrong with me for asking, they too turned me down.

So, I gave up. And that turned out to be brilliant. Two days before the prom, I inexplicably got three invitations from (otherwise) quite respectable and pretty young ladies. To this day, I don't know why. But it was yet another successful hunting strategy. You don't stalk deer when you can sit in a stand and wait for them to come to you.

Chapter Nineteen

PALE FACES

As a kid, I was the victim of an hereditary curse my Mom called "face aches". She said it was caused by telling too many lies. I have since learned it is a chronic inflammation of the superior sinus cavities. (I had no idea some sinus cavities were better than others.) Anyway, the condition became worse with age. By the time I was in High School, it was unbearable in that I had missed a couple of fishing trips because of the pain. Now, I didn't mind missing school, baptisms, or part-time jobs, but fishing? I took myself to the doctor.

After explaining my symptoms to the nurse, she said my condition sounded like a deviated septum. I didn't have a clue what a deviated septum was, but being a teenager, I was reluctant to make a fool of myself in front of a pretty woman. I just said, "Thought so".

The doctor examined me and confirmed the nurse's diagnosis. In a nasal twang that would have made Willie Nelson jealous, he said, "you have a deviated theptum".

"A what?" I inquired, incredulously.

"Deviated theptum", he repeated, annoyed.

"What's that?" I asked anxiously.

"Crooked noth bone", he whined. "Nothing to worry about. I have one too."

I usually didn't ask doctors a lot of questions. I was afraid of my ignorance and scared of their answers. (Still am.) But since he was a specialist and I was tired of missing fishing trips, I pressed my luck.

"What do we do about a crooked noth, I mean nose bone?" I cringed.

"Operation", the good doctor replied.

"Have you had it done?"

"Oh, no!" he said, distressed. "Much too painful!"

I got up and left.

My loathing of pain and fear of doctors who were invariably associated with that pain was only just beginning. When I was a senior, I managed to drive a catfish pectoral fin half-way through my palm. I shortly found myself in a doctor's waiting room, in deep pain and dreading the needles that were to come. As a devout coward regarding anything to do with foreign objects entering my body and only minutes away from the actual event, my terror went into full bloom.

My knees began to quake noticeably and uncontrollable trembling overtook my hands and arms. Such was the severity of my shaking that the little bell by the nurses' station began to tinkle lightly. People noticed.

When my face turned the color of, oh, I don't know, the cloroxed handkerchief with which I was mopping my brow, a 90-year-old lady, a guy with both legs in casts and a pregnant woman got up and offered me their seats. Of course the proper thing to do would have been to graciously decline their offers, but the old lady looked like she was in pretty good shape.

Shame of cowardice is overrated. We are all scared of something. And it's not just physical harm and pain. (And if you are a fan of the outdoors, you are going to experience plenty of that.) We are scared of being different; of failure; of events that are not even likely to take place. That is why we have antiperspirant, aspirin and insurance. We all fear. It helps run the economy. I am not ashamed of my phobias involving snakes or heights or one-eyed kindergarten teachers.

But I still have face aches. So on the other hand, my Mom might have been right. Maybe I did tell too many lies as a kid.

Chapter Twenty

RED FACES

Have you ever noticed that the older you become, the more you forget? It's true. Some wise person told me that once. I don't remember who it was. After you hit 60 or so, short term memory is completely gone, like an eight pound bass on four pound test. But for some insidious reason, certain vestiges of long term memory remain. You will never forget life's most embarrassing moments.

For instance, when I was in high school and free for the summer, I went to work for a department store to save up for a nifty little 14 foot jon boat and a two horse outboard. My co-worker and I had just brought a very expensive sofa into a very rich lady's house. She was having a "social" and the room was filled with over-dressed, high-classed, country club ladies. They ooohed and aaahhhed at the expensive, elegant and tasteful piece of furniture we were delivering. Of course, they ignored we blue-jeaned, sneaker-clad ruffians who delivered it. I put a stop to that.

As we were exiting to the patio to bring in the matching love seat, I walked directly into a closed plate-glass sliding door. The sounds of the initial impact of my face on the door followed immediately by my butt on the floor (Wham! Thunk!) Was followed by a deafening silence. It was what I supposed deep space would sound like. (I did see stars.)

But it wasn't so much the silence in which I was enveloped, as the feeling on the back of my neck that this crowd of Southern sophisticated women were ogling me in sheer disbelief that anyone could be so stupid. The rule was that the hired help was supposed to be only peripherally visible and completely silent. I was neither.

I could physically feel, without looking, the stares over their tiny bifocals and monocles dropping from their widening eyes. I knew their mouths were open and their cocktails frozen in midair. I also knew that I had proven beyond a shadow of a doubt their unspoken theory that I was but little removed from homo erectus (actually being homo pronus at the time). After what I am sure was several hours of silence, the hostess said politely, "Young mayan, ah you awlright?" "Yes ma'am", I replied. "You use Windex, don't you?"

That same summer, not having yet saved up enough for my treasured boat and motor, I was working on the loading dock of the aforementioned department store. (They had decided to keep me away from public scrutiny.) The personnel manager had taken an interest in me for some reason and he had been trying to talk me into continuing to work on the weekends after school started again. I feigned interest, knowing full well as soon as I had the money, my weekends were going to be spent fishing in my new boat. The Lord punished me for that.

One day, the manager brought the chain store's visiting CEO down to the dock to meet us peons. I was quite taken by surprise at the introduction of this demi-god. As we shook hands, my mind raced. Should I be formal and say, "How do you do?" Or should I be cool and say "Howzit goin'?" What came out was "How do you goo?" I never saw either of them again.

I did save up enough for the little boat, but I never conquered my predilection for embarrassing myself. And selective memory is a terrible thing. I don't remember my senior English teacher's name. But I remember falling down the stairs with an armload of books headed to her class and landing at the feet of the head cheerleader. And I don't know how I could have possibly mispronounced "brazier" on a live student radio advertisement.

I don't know what possessed me to have beans and franks before my first drive-in movie date. I don't remember the name of the movie, but I remember with perfect clarity the words, "What on earth is that?" I learned a great lesson that night. "Oh, that's some bream I forgot to take out of the trunk." Blame it on the fish. Always blame it on the fish.

Chapter Twenty Two

HISSSS

It was one of those Southern Spring afternoons that Henry David Thoreau could wax philosophical about for hours. Ducky Jones and I, teenage lads at the time, were plying the banks of a calm, pastoral pond in an 8 foot pram, fly fishing for bluegill. We found a good spot and eased our concrete block anchor overboard silently. The only sound was the soft swish of our rhythmic casts.

One could only appreciate what happened next if one has been awakened from a sound sleep by a maniac dismantling one's bed with a chainsaw. A world record bullfrog leapt from the bank 30 feet away, bellowing (yes, bellowing) at the top of its lungs, hit the water once and landed in the bottom of our little craft. The adrenaline rush of having a 5 pound, shrieking amphibian jump into the boat was immediately followed by a secondary and more powerful rush when we spied the object of its terror.

Writhing off of the bank was the biggest, blackest, fattest, thickest water moccasin in the Western Hemisphere. It was obscene. It came off of the bank and came off of the bank and came off the bank and by the time it was half way to our flimsy pram, we still hadn't seen its tail. The premise was simple. The frog was in the boat. The snake wanted the frog. It would eat anything that got in its way.

I don't remember if there was a conscious mental decision or if basic primal instinct just took over, but we did the only obvious thing to do. We screamed obscenities and paddled with all our might. We covered the 100 or so yards back to the landing in a time-distance ratio that would have baffled a physicist. Ducky had let out the patented screeching quack for which he was nicknamed when we spotted the morbid freak and I don't think he took a breath until the boat touched land.

We sat there a moment. The only sound was our labored breathing. We pondered with disbelief what had just happened. We had paddled the entire length of the pond with a fly rod and a baseball cap. Dragging a 12 pound anchor. I don't know what happened to the paddle. Perhaps we threw it at the monster. Perhaps the frog threw it. Somewhere along the way, the frog had abandoned ship, coward that he was. I can't really blame him though. The decibel level must have reached an horrendous volume.

As we sat there, Ducky in the stern and I in the bow, gasping for air, I was witness to a scientific phenomenon I had neither seen before nor since. It involved the space-time continuum. We had tied to the back of the boat a small stringer of bluegill. They had probably become airborne at some point in our journey but were now recovering and began splashing immediately behind Ducky.

One second, we were on opposite ends of the boat, facing each other. The next second, he was sitting by my side. As many times as I have replayed that scene in my mind, I do not remember, for the life of me, seeing him move. We sat awhile, side by side, staring out across the water, watching a flock of mallards Ducky had inadvertently called up. It was good to be alive. That pond may still be there. I wouldn't know.

Chapter Twenty Three

WHATEVER HAPPENED TO RANDOLF SCOTT?

A line from an old Statler Brothers song asks, "Whatever happened to Randolf Scott, ridin' the trails alone?" Since I was born shortly after the Industrial Revolution and there have been lots of changes in my lifetime, I wonder about stuff like that now too. Not about Randolf Scott (since he would be about 130 years old now, I assume he rode into the sunset long ago), but about how fishing has changed since I was a lad.

Hunting hasn't changed much. We still go into the woods and fields and take game just like ol' Dan'l Boone did. Guns haven't changed much in the last 100 years. If someone asked me, "Whatever happened to that old Krag-Jorgenson you used to deer hunt with?" (I don't think even the Statler Brothers could make a hit out of that), I would reply that it's still on the gun rack in my den and I still deer hunt with it. It's a model 1898 .30-40 with an appendage on the side for a saddle strap. Without that little piece of metal, it is basically the same as any rifle that came out of the factory this year.

Oh, there have been a few modifications in firearms. They came up with the downward shell ejection. I didn't much care if a hot casing went down the collar of the guy on my right. But now, as improbable as it is, I have to worry about one going down the front of my pants. And they have replaced wood with plastic, but nothing earth shattering. Technically, shells are still loaded with smokeless powder. Not much new there. And game animals certainly haven't changed. Deer still see me before I see them and doves can still fly faster than I can fire my 20 gauge. But fishing and fishing gear and fish have changed dramatically.

For instance, whatever happened to stupid bass? The first bait casting outfit I ever used was spooled with black braided nylon line so thick a WWF champ would rupture himself trying to break it. A fish could see it 30 feet away in muddy water. But I still caught stupid bass with it. I got many of them on an old Sonic. It was a yellow lipless crank bait with a black lightning bolt emblazoned on each side. I've studied baitfish for many years and have never seen one whose scales looked like the symbol for electricity.

Whatever happened to rubber worms? Not plastic. Rubber. They had the flexibility of a small stick, but they were virtually indestructible and I caught lots of stupid bass on them. And unless you had an obsessive compulsive disorder, making decisions was much easier back then, because rubber worms only came in two colors: black and red. And since you could barely pull them off the hook with a pair of pliers, you only had to have a couple. If, on the off-chance one tore, you simply held a match to it, pressed the sides together, and viola! Brand new, though slightly discolored, rubber worm.

Whatever happened to trading coupons for fishing gear? My Dad smoked cigars and saved the little bands wrapped around each stogie until he had enough to send in for rods, reels, tackle boxes, minnow buckets, etc. All via the U.S. Postal Service. And we're talking name brand quality merchandise. He outfitted the whole family. But that stuff is so expensive today, you would die of lung cancer before you got a cricket cage.

Whatever happened to snake bite kits? They were little cylinders made from hard rubber (probably left over from the worm molds) that pulled apart to make two suction cups. Inside was a tourniquet, a razor blade and a set of instructions. The latter were so lengthy and complicated that you would have succumbed to the venom long before you finished reading them. But basically, they directed you to tie off the affected limb above the bite with the shoestring provided, make "x" incisions on the bite marks, and use the suction cups to eliminate the poison.

Exactly all the things we now know not to do. Anyone who actually used the kit would have probably gone into shock, bled to death or set the stage for future amputation. But having one in your tackle box gave you a sense of security, false or not. Had I ever been bitten though, I am sure the snake bite kit would have never even crossed my mind. I would have screamed and ran in directionless terror until I collapsed and died.

Whatever happened to fishing cars? Not everybody had one, but they were fairly common. Of course, everyone had a family sedan or station wagon, but sometimes Dad and/or his teenage son would rescue a 20 year old clunker from the junkyard and get it running. It was beat to hell anyway, so you didn't mind taking it across cow pastures or down logging roads or through creeks to get to your favorite fishing hole. Hence, "fishin' car."

But parents of teenagers also used them for birth control devices. They would only let their sons or daughters go out on a date if they went in a fishing car. The idea was that it was difficult to get romantic in a vehicle with dried fish scales stuck on the backrests and the occasional #6 bream hook embedded in the upholstery. And the odor of dead crickets and rotting redworms wafting from the glove compartment or back floorboard.

Fishing cars, by their very nature, were forever breaking down, so everyone had a few tools under the front seat. My friend Ducky Jones had a 1940's something Nash and his tools consisted of a screwdriver, a pair of pliers and a hammer. His girlfriend called them a turner, a pincher and a pounder. God bless him, Ducky loved them dumb. When his Nash quit running, for some reason still unbeknownst to me, it responded well to a few well placed smacks of the hammer to the engine block.

One night, while we were on a double date, the old Nash quit and we coasted to a stop. Ducky's girlfriend turned to him and said, "Well, I guess you better pull out your pounder". In the back seat, my date and I looked at each other incredulously. It took a few moments for the implications of that particular suggestion to register. Shortly thereafter, he became known around school as Lucky Ducky.

Whatever happened to those huge top water lures? Today, we measure the weight of lures in ounces. Way back when, I think they measured them in pounds. I remember having a Lucky 13, a Torpedo and a Jitterbug that I know were 6 inches long and were outfitted with three sets of welded treble hooks they use today for mako shark fishing. I suppose they went the way of stupid bass.

Whatever happened to wooden boats, steel spinning rods and porcupine quill floats? I wonder about stuff like that. And I wonder, whatever *did* happen to Randolf Scott?

ABOUT THE AUTHOR

Garry was born in Montgomery, Alabama in 1946 and completed two professional careers in central Alabama. He worked as a high school classroom teacher and administrator for 20 years and then served as a deputy sheriff for 21 years. He was also a member of the Army National Guard for 6 years. During these tenures, he simultaneously wrote editorials and sports columns for three weekly newspapers.

Garry received his Bachelor's degree from Troy University; a Master's degree from Auburn University and POST certification from the University of Alabama.

He is the author of a published non-fiction history book entitled *Slavery and the Civil War – What Your History Teacher Didn't Tell You* (Shotwell Publications, 2018). He is also the co-author and illustrator of a children's chapbook entitled *You Can't Hide a Hippo*. Since retirement, he writes feature stories for two outdoor magazines.

The author may be contacted via the U.S. Postal Service at 19 Lilac Lane, Montgomery, AL 36109.

Available From Shotwell Publishing

If you enjoyed this book, perhaps some of our other titles will pique your interest. The following titles are now available for your reading pleasure… Enjoy!

MARK C. ATKINS

WOMEN IN COMBAT
Feminism Goes to War

JOYCE BENNETT

MARYLAND, MY MARYLAND
The Cultural Cleansing of a Small Southern State

GARRY BOWERS

SLAVERY AND THE CIVIL WAR
What Your History Teacher Didn't Tell You

DIXIE DAYS
Reminiscences Of A Southern Boyhood

JERRY BREWER

DISMANTLING THE REPUBLIC

ANDREW P. CALHOUN, JR.

MY OWN DARLING WIFE
Letters from a Confederate Volunteer

JOHN CHODES

SEGREGATION
Federal Policy or Racism?

WASHINGTON'S KKK
The Union League during Southern Reconstruction

PAUL C. GRAHAM

CONFEDERAPHOBIA
An American Epidemic

WHEN THE YANKEES COME
Former South Carolina Slaves Remember Sherman's Invasion

JOSEPH JAY

SACRED CONVICTION
The South's Stand for Biblical Authority

SUZANNE PARFITT JOHNSON

MAXCY GREGG'S SPORTING
JOURNALS 1842 - 1858

JAMES RONALD KENNEDY

DIXIE RISING: Rules for Rebels

WHEN REBEL WAS COOL
Growing Up in Dixie, 1950-1965

JAMES R. & WALTER D. KENNEDY

PUNISHED WITH POVERTY
The Suffering South – Prosperity to Poverty and the Continuing Struggle, 2nd ed.

THE SOUTH WAS RIGHT!
A New Edition For The 21st Century

YANKEE EMPIRE
Aggressive Abroad and Despotic at Home

PHILIP LEIGH

THE DEVIL'S TOWN
Hot Springs During the Gangster Era

U.S. GRANT'S FAILED PRESIDENCY

CAUSES OF THE CIVIL WAR

LEWIS LIBERMAN

SNOWFLAKE BUDDIES
ABC Leftism for Kids!

JACK MARQUARDT

AROUND THE WORLD
IN EIGHTY YEARS
Confessions of a Connecticut Confederate

MICHAEL MARTIN

SOUTHERN GRIT
Sensing the Siege at Petersburg

SAMUEL W. MITCHAM

THE GREATEST LYNCHING IN AMERICAN HISTORY: New York, 1863

CHARLES T. PACE

LINCOLN AS HE REALLY WAS

SOUTHERN INDEPENDENCE. WHY WAR?
The War to Prevent Southern Independence

JAMES RUTLEDGE ROESCH

FROM FOUNDING FATHERS TO FIRE EATERS
The Constitutional Doctrine of States' Rights in the Old South

KIRKPATRICK SALE

EMANCIPATION HELL
The Tragedy Wrought by Lincoln's Emancipation Proclamation

KAREN STOKES

A LEGION OF DEVILS
Sherman in South Carolina

CAROLINA LOVE LETTERS

LESLIE R. TUCKER

OLD TIMES THERE SHOULD NOT BE FORGOTTEN
Cultural Genocide in Dixie

JOHN VINSON

SOUTHERNER, TAKE YOUR STAND!
Reclaim Your Identity. Reclaim your Life.

HOWARD RAY WHITE

HOW SOUTHERN FAMILIES MADE AMERICA
Colonization, Revolution, and Expansion From Virginia Colony to the Republic of Texas 1607 to 1836

UNDERSTANDING CREATION AND EVOLUTION

CLYDE N. WILSON

LIES MY TEACHER TOLD ME
The True History of the War for Southern Independence & Other Essays

THE OLD SOUTH
50 Essential Books
(Southern Reader's Guide 1)

THE WAR BETWEEN THE STATES
60 Essential Books
(Southern Reader's Guide 2)

RECONSTRUCTION AND THE NEW SOUTH, 1865-1913
50 Essential Books
(Southern Reader's Guide 3)

THE YANKEE PROBLEM
An American Dilemma
(The Wilson Files 1)

NULLIFICATION
Reclaiming the Consent of the Governed
(The Wilson Files 1I)

ANNALS OF THE STUPID PARTY
Republicans Before Trump
(The Wilson Files 1II)

JOE A. WOLVERTON, II

"WHAT DEGREE OF MADNESS?"
Madison's Method to Make American STATES Again

WALTER KIRK WOOD

BEYOND SLAVERY
The Northern Romantic Nationalist Origins of America's Civil War

GREEN ALTAR BOOKS
(Literary Imprint)

CATHARINE SAVAGE BROSMAN
AN AESTHETIC EDUCATION
and Other Stories

CHAINED TREE, CHAINED OWLS:
Poems

RANDALL IVEY
A NEW ENGLAND ROMANCE
and Other SOUTHERN Stories

JAMES EVERETT KIBLER
TILLER

THOMAS MOORE
A FATAL MERCY
The Man Who Lost The Civil War

KAREN STOKES
BELLES
A Carolina Love Story

CAROLINA TWILIGHT

HONOR IN THE DUST

THE IMMORTALS

THE SOLDIER'S GHOST
A Tale of Charleston

WILLIAM A. THOMAS, JR.
RUNAWAY HALEY
An Imagined Family Saga

GOLD-BUG
(Mystery & Suspense Imprint)

MICHAEL ANDREW GRISSOM
BILLIE JO

BRANDI PERRY
SPLINTERED
A New Orleans Tale

MARTIN L. WILSON
TO JEKYLL AND HIDE

Free Book Offer

Sign-up for new release notifications and receive a **FREE** downloadable edition of *Lies My Teacher Told Me: The True History of the War for Southern Independence* by Dr. Clyde N. Wilson and *Confederaphobia: An American Epidemic* by Paul C. Graham by visiting FreeLiesBook.com. You can always unsubscribe and keep the book, so you've got nothing to lose!

www.ingramcontent.com/pod-product-compliance
Lightning Source LLC
LaVergne TN
LVHW020937090426
835512LV00020B/3394